Donald G. Hanway, DMin

A Theology of Gay and Lesbian Inclusion
Love Letters to the Church

Pre-publication
REVIEWS,
COMMENTARIES,
EVALUATIONS . . .

D0149005

"Hanway is a seasoned minister, profound thinker, and clear writer. His book is compassionate, erudite, and well reasoned. His letters make a historical Christian tradition new and apt for the twenty-first century. His topic—the inclusion of gays and lesbians in the church community—is important and timely."

Mary Pipher, PhD
Author, *Writing to Change the World*

"Would an accessible, scripturally based, commonsense book on the issues of human sexuality be helpful in your community? If so, then this new book by Donald Hanway may be just what you have been looking for. Growing out of his long tenure as a pastor, this work is based on a theology of experience. It invites people to rethink their own fears or prejudices by looking at them through the eyes of Jesus. In fact, Jesus is ever-present in this book as the model for what radical acceptance and love can be like. Donald Hanway writes in a conversational way that is ideal for any person who comes to his topic with some trepidation. His effort is to reassure people that our differences, even our differences in sexual attitudes, do not have to divide us or make us anxious. Instead, through the unconditional love of God, we can all find our place at the Lord's table. This balanced message of hope is a powerful antidote to much of the frenzied rhetoric we often hear when Christians start to talk about sex. It is a timely, useful, and overdue word of calm and compassion."

The Right Reverend Steven Charleston
President and Dean,
Episcopal Divinity School

The Haworth Pastoral Press®
An Imprint of The Haworth Press, Inc.
New York • London • Oxford

NOTES FOR PROFESSIONAL LIBRARIANS AND LIBRARY USERS

This is an original book title published by The Haworth Pastoral Press®, and imprint of The Haworth Press, Inc. Unless otherwise noted in specific chapters with attribution, materials in this book have not been previously published elsewhere in any format or language.

CONSERVATION AND PRESERVATION NOTES

All books published by The Haworth Press, Inc., and its imprints are printed on certified pH neutral, acid-free book grade paper. This paper meets the minimum requirements of American National Standard for Information Sciences-Permanence of Paper for Printed Material, ANSI Z39.48-1984.

DIGITAL OBJECT IDENTIFIER (DOI) LINKING

The Haworth Press is participating in reference linking for elements of our original books. (For more information on reference linking initiatives, please consult the CrossRef Web site at www.crossref.org.) When citing an element of this book such as a chapter, include the element's Digital Object Identifier (DOI) as the last item of the reference. A Digital Object Identifier is a persistent, authoritative, and unique identifier that a publisher assigns to each element of a book. Because of its persistence, DOIs will enable The Haworth Press and other publishers to link to the element referenced, and the link will not break over time. This will be a great resource in scholarly research.

A Theology of Gay and Lesbian Inclusion
Love Letters to the Church

A Theology of Gay and Lesbian Inclusion
Love Letters to the Church

Donald G. Hanway, DMin

The Haworth Pastoral Press®
An Imprint of The Haworth Press, Inc.
New York • London • Oxford

For more information on this book or to order, visit
http://www.haworthpress.com/store/product.asp?sku=5661

or call 1-800-HAWORTH (800-429-6784) in the United States and Canada
or (607) 722-5857 outside the United States and Canada

or contact orders@HaworthPress.com

Published by

The Haworth Pastoral Press®, an imprint of The Haworth Press, Inc., 10 Alice Street, Binghamton, NY 13904-1580.

PUBLISHER'S NOTE
The development, preparation, and publication of this work has been undertaken with great care. However, the Publisher, employees, editors, and agents of The Haworth Press are not responsible for any errors contained herein or for consequences that may ensue from use of materials or information contained in this work. The Haworth Press is committed to the dissemination of ideas and information according to the highest standards of intellectual freedom and the free exchange of ideas. Statements made and opinions expressed in this publication do not necessarily reflect the views of the Publisher, Directors, management, or staff of The Haworth Press, Inc., or an endorsement by them.

Identities and circumstances of individuals discussed in this book have been changed to protect confidentiality.

Cover design by Jennifer M. Gaska.

Library of Congress Cataloging-in-Publication Data

Hanway, D. G. (Donald Grant)
    A theology of gay and lesbian inclusion : love letters to the church / Donald G. Hanway.
        p. cm.
    Includes index.
    ISBN-13: 978-0-7890-2998-0 (hard : alk. paper)
    ISBN-10: 0-7890-2998-7 (hard : alk. paper)
    ISBN-13: 978-0-7890-2999-7 (soft : alk. paper)
    ISBN-10: 0-7890-2999-5 (soft : alk. paper)
    1. Homosexuality—Religious aspects—Christianity. 2. Gays—Religious life. 3. Liberation theology. I. Title.

BR115.H6H36 2006
261.8'35766—dc22
                                                                          2005030755

In memory of my friend Sheila,
and all those brave gay souls
who have taught me so much about
love and courage.

Do not remember the former things, or consider the things of old. I am about to do a new thing; now it springs forth, do you not perceive it? (Isa. 43:18-19)

Is not this the fast that I choose: to loose the bonds of injustice, to undo the thongs of the yoke, to let the oppressed go free, and to break every yoke? (Isa. 58:6)

Blessed are those who are persecuted for righteousness' sake, for theirs is the kingdom of heaven. (Matt. 5:10)

CONTENTS

ABOUT THE AUTHOR

The **Rev. Dr. Don Hanway** is an Episcopal priest, recently retired after thirty-two years of parish ministry. After receiving degrees in psychology and philosophy from the University of Nebraska–Lincoln, he attended seminary in Virginia and served congregations in Michigan and Nebraska. Married for forty years to Nan Kingman, he is father of Laura, Stephen, and Julie; grandfather of Nathan, Alex, Corinne, Elena, Calvin, and "Mr. T." His hobbies include cinema, golf, and letter-writing.

Preface

Whoever you are, I salute your courage. It takes courage even to look at a book that goes against the cultural tide of prejudice—especially prejudice that wears robes of holiness and tradition. It takes courage to contemplate the possibility of changing your mind, of admitting that what you have been handed as gospel up to now is simply not true. If you are gay, it takes courage to stand up for who you are, and if you are Christian as well, it takes courage to say, "I believe in God, and I know that in God's eyes I deserve better than what the Church has so far seen fit to call the Good News—for I, too, am a child of God."

This book is for people of courage and honesty, but especially for those who are members of the Church, and who therefore carry the responsibility of being ambassadors of the Good News: the Good News that God in Christ has proclaimed God's love for *all* people—not a second-class love for some and a first-class love for the voting majority, but a first-class love for all.

The purpose of this book is to equip you, Christian warrior of the Gospel of peace, to stand against those who use the Bible to resist change—even that change of which our Lord would approve. In one sense, nothing is revolutionary in this book. It is a book grounded in the Bible. It is a book that respects tradition—up to a point: that point where tradition has to change, to give way to what the Holy Spirit is showing us in our day of the mind of Christ. This is not revolutionary, because tradition has had to change before; it is a developing truth, born of the corporate experience of the children of God and open to our claiming the right to exercise our God-given gift of reason.

This book may or may not change you. It may only confirm what you already know or have been coming to suspect. It is not an academic book. There are no footnotes. All references are

doi:10.1300/5661_a

contained within the body of the text. It is a book of permission, and it is my personal testimony and witness to the truth I have come to know. I welcome you as a fellow pilgrim in search of the truth. Notice I use a small "t," for while we are on our lifelong journey, we are seekers in quest of, but not yet fully in possession of, the Truth. God does, indeed, reveal truth to those who are ready to receive it, but this truth is not contained solely within the pages of the Bible. It is a living word, which has come among us and continues to live within us. It is a word of kinship, of recognition. It is a word that sets us all free.

God bless you, Christian seeker and truth-teller.

Acknowledgments

Thanks are due to my initial readers, especially Steve Buhler, Peter Allman, Pamela Starr, Lynn Samsel, and Joe Hahn, for all their helpful suggestions, and to Glenda Hinz, my expert typist. Thanks to my parents for teaching me about the values that matter.

Thanks to my many encouragers, including Mary Pipher, Jean Harvey, Kelly Grey Carlisle, Kim Heald, Joe Burnett, Andi Boyd, my wife Nan, and the people of St. Mark's on the Campus. Thanks for an assist to two "earth angels," Gary Gabelhouse and Tom Frye.

Special thanks to my interviewees, who remain anonymous. I salute them for their openness and generosity.

doi:10.1300/5661_b

Letter 1

Letter of Introduction

Dear Prospective Reader:

"I love you. Is that okay?"—God
For my last few years as a parish priest and college chaplain, I had that message on my bulletin board. It's the Bible in brief, and it's also what I want to say to you.

I love you—though my love is derivative and imperfect. I love you because God has loved me, and love isn't a gift one can keep to oneself. Whoever you are, I am convinced that God loves you too, and God wants to enrich your life by loving others through you. We need a lot more love in this world.

I'm writing to you because I believe in you, and I believe in the Holy Spirit. I believe that most people want to do the right thing, once they know what that is. Knowing the right thing to do depends to a great degree on how you understand God.

When I was in eighth grade, our Sunday school class was taught for a time by a young graduate student in philosophy. One day he challenged us by asking, "How do you know there is a God?" Finally we turned the question back on him: "How do *you* know?" He said, "I know there is a God, because I have him at home in a bottle." That baffled us, and he offered no explanation. Perhaps he wanted us to think about it. I'm asking you to do something similar: Not to think about *whether* God exists, but about the *nature* of God, and how your view of God affects the way you treat other people.

Asking what we think about God is a question nearly always worth considering again. What we learned about God in Sunday

doi:10.1300/5661_01

1

school may not be adequate to the complexities of adult life. Many voices have presumed, and are presuming, to speak for the Church universal. It may be that you have not yet heard some voices you need to hear.

The Church is floundering right now and not because it is divided. The Church in this world will always be divided, both on many small points that do not really matter, and on some large ones that really do. The Church is floundering because many sincere and well-meaning Christians have been misinformed or are currently in a state of confusion about what is true and what is important, about what needs preserving and what needs changing. I'm writing in an effort to dispel some of that misinformation and confusion by telling some true stories, including my own. I'm writing because I have lived my life inside the Church and still love her, even though in some ways I know her too well. In spite of her many flaws, she is still the Body of Christ and the Bride of Christ.

At the age of sixty, I am newly retired from full-time ministry. Over the span of more than three decades in ordained ministry, I have learned a lot about human nature, as well as about God's goodness. Among the many who have been my teachers are faithful men and women who happen to be homosexual. Their orientation was not chosen, as though it were a "lifestyle." Life dealt them a challenging hand, and these people I know have played it about as well as anyone could. I want to tell a bit of their stories. However, their stories are only part of a larger one, which I think the Church needs to hear. It is a story about what matters most, and how we can lose that if we aren't careful.

The Church is floundering because many other stories are being told and uncritically received—stories that disagree with the one I am going to tell. My wife, who has listened to me preach for thirty-two years, likes that story of "God in a bottle" well enough that she tells it herself every now and then. For her, it's a reminder of how easy and how tempting it is to think we have God figured out, or to think that God can be domesticated to support our puny presumptions of reality.

I believe in the Holy Spirit, who is God among us, not domesticated at all. God did not stop communicating in the first century, when the last writings in the sacred canon were composed. God is always communicating with us. We are not always able to hear or willing to listen. There *is* Truth with a capital "T," but it does not belong to us. Our little truths are at best approximations, stages on our journey to where we will finally meet the Truth face to face.

It is the spirit of the living God who brings to life the words of holy scripture and convinces us of the truth of what God is doing in our lives today. I am willing to trust you, dear reader, to listen to the Holy Spirit speaking in your own heart, and then to decide whether what I am telling you is true and important—even, perhaps, most important of all.

Why am I presenting this message as a series of letters? In the early Church, pastors wrote to believers near and far to encourage them, to strengthen their relationship with the wider Church, and to remind them of teachings in peril of being lost, as well as to answer questions and to correct misunderstandings. My reasons include those purposes, as well as the fact that I enjoy writing letters—it's comfortable and natural for me. I will not be making an academic argument, but a personal appeal. I am asking you personally to listen to the Holy Spirit and then to do the right thing.

I am passionate about the stories I have to tell. I agree with Christians telling stories opposing mine on one key point at least: The integrity of the Church and the integrity of the gospel *is* at stake. How the Church deals with gay and lesbian people is a test case in our day for fidelity to the message of Jesus Christ.

What my experience has equipped me to do is to provide a working rationale or theology for the many faithful church members who have not had the time or taken the time to work out for themselves all the implications of the present situation, in which some old assumptions about God and the Bible are being challenged, and rightfully so. If I learned anything in getting the second of my four academic degrees, an MA in philosophy, it is to take a close look at the hidden, gratuitous assumptions that so often and so easily slide in under the radar at the beginning or during the course of an argument. Most faulty conclusions arise not so much from faulty logic as from assumptions that are blurred, slippery, or flat-out wrong. Why do such assumptions pass without challenge? Because people give them the benefit of the doubt and never go back to look at them more closely, and because those who make use of them are more focused on an end to be served than on the veracity of the means employed to arrive there.

I'm also aware that another mechanism is often at work, which may be stated in this way: "Don't bother me with any new facts; my mind is already made up." Most of us resist changing familiar patterns of thinking and behaving, especially as we get older. It's too much effort, especially when there doesn't seem to be any reward.

So this book is for you, earnest church member—and for you, if you are among the many who are *not* currently drawn to the Church. Perhaps you hope the Church might become more than it has been. Perhaps you long for a church more in touch with the pain and needs of people today. Perhaps you yearn for a church more willing to engage the unpleasant truths of how power is wielded, and how the Church has so often been an accomplice to injustice.

This book is for you and your own process of reasoning—but also for Frank*, now age seventy, who recently wrote to me:

> I am not ashamed to be gay. I did not choose it, but I accept it. All I ask is to be treated equally and be given the same equal rights as heterosexuals. I want to be liked for who I am and what I contribute. . . .

This book is for you, and for Jesus, and also for Elena, who told me in an interview this past year: "Many, many gay and lesbian people have a church-shaped wound: they have a steeple hole in their hearts."

This book is for you, and for Rory, who told me, "Before I knew that I was gay, I both knew that I was gay and knew that I was *not* gay—I *couldn't* be gay, because that was mental illness."

---

*All interviewees' names have been changed to protect their privacy.

This book is for you, and for all the people you love and don't love, and for Michael, who gave ten years of his life in vain attempts to change his sexual orientation, under the earnest tutelage of well-meaning Christians, and who now says, "I don't know *what* I believe anymore, about God or the Bible."

Here is a quick overview of these letters, followed by a personal summary of what the Gospel means to me, so that you can decide if we are talking about the same subject, and so that you may begin to grasp why I want the Church to be passionate about the Gospel as well. I think the logic of my order of presentation will become evident.

After this letter of introduction, I describe, as well as I can, what is at the heart of our faith as Christians. Then I write about what love means and what gets in its way. I'll be talking about sin, but not necessarily in the way many are accustomed to thinking about it.

From there I write about both sides of the Church—its human side and its divine side. Then I address a huge topic that the Church has barely begun to address—the gift of human sexuality, how we view it and deal with it, and how it relates to spirituality.

In two letters, I share some stories of gay and lesbian people—how they have suffered at the hands of the proclaimers of God's love, and what their "agenda," as some have called it, actually is.

No book about the Church and homosexual people is complete without some discussion of what the Bible says, what it doesn't say, and what it assumes. After this discussion, I set forth a biblically based outline of ethics for Christians, as a way to bring some clarity out of the prevailing confusion. All biblical quotations in this book are from the New Revised Standard Version (NRSV).

Finally, I appeal to the Church, including you, dear reader. I ask you to decide whether what I have shared is cogent and compelling, and I urge you to follow your decision by writing your own love letters on behalf of the Good News that truly is good news for all people.

Here in brief is what I have come to believe, after many years of servant ministry, study, teaching, and preaching; thirty-seven years as a husband; thirty-two years as a father; six years as a grandfather; and approximately forty-six years since my hormones kicked in and I became a flaming heterosexual. I'm setting forth this personal testament in hopes that you may decide that we are not so very far apart in what we think is true and important. Here is what I believe about life and love and the fundamental reality in this universe and beyond.

My Testament

Life begins and ends beyond the curtain of our comprehension. We come out of mystery and move toward mystery. Yet within that all-encompassing mystery we dare to address as personal, there is light.

The essential message of Christianity is stated eloquently in the prologue of the Gospel according to St. John (John 1:1-18), where the evangelist sums up his own witness and gives voice to what has come to be called the doctrine of the incarnation, God taking human flesh, as in these verses: "The true light, which enlightens everyone, was coming into the world" (John 1:9). . . . "And the Word became flesh and lived among us, and we have seen his glory, the glory as of a father's only son, full of grace and truth" (John 1:14).

My view of reality is that the origin of that light and that word embraces all living beings, conscious and unconscious, believing and unbelieving, bathing them in a generous energy we can best describe as unconditional love. As a Christian, I subscribe to the truth of incarnation, the underlying message of Christmas, and am bold to say that Jesus of Nazareth was and is the living embodiment of that light and that word. He articulated in his life, death, and resurrection the nature and intent of what we call divine, and also what it means to be fully human. He showed us what it means to love and to grasp the significance of our lives.

The Church as an organism human and divine flows out of the person and message of Jesus. The human side of the Church, as oppressive as that often can be, is forgivable in the long run because Jesus embraced all people, even in their sinfulness, and chose to work through any who responded, in whatever degree, to his message. The Church is divine because it is an extension of the incarnation; it is, for better or worse, the body of Christ in this world, constantly in need of redemption, yet carrying also within its life the means of redemption.

The proper work of the Church is sharing the message of Jesus by living that message and sharing the life of Jesus by extending the benefits of loving community to an ever-wider circle. In my own tradition, which is both catholic and reformed, living in community involves gathering around the altar (a sign of the sacrifice of Jesus) to share the sacraments, which are signs of the life of the risen Lord in our midst.

The word "gospel" means more than just a record of the life and message of Jesus, and more than just preserving an essential truth. Our word "gospel" comes from a Greek word meaning "good news," and the only way we can preserve the essential truth of that message is by retaining what is good and life-giving about it. Sadly, the way the Gospel has been preached and practiced has made it extremely *bad* news to many. It is an irony that might be laughable, were it not so horrifically sad, that the word which is life and light has brought the death of hope to many who have found themselves excluded by human arbiters speaking in the name of the almighty. The ultimate irony, if anything in this world can be described as ultimate, is that the spokespersons of love are often the most unloving of all.

I believe that all who dare to speak on behalf of the Good News—including myself—must know their own blindness, their own denials and perversions of the Good News, the "log" in their own eyes (Luke 6:41-42), their own tendencies to justify themselves while denouncing others, and their own reluctance to listen to those who would point out their blind spots and their areas of willing ignorance to the pain of their fellow human beings. In short, all who would be purveyors of the Good News must be users of the Good News, not on the one-time basis of "I've seen the light," but on a daily basis of repentance, openness to new learning, and the deeply held conviction that love is greater than any of its denials.

I believe that sin as refusal to love is more pervasive than anyone in the Church would like to admit, yet is ultimately unable to separate us from a loving God. In other words, I believe that love has won and will win, against all detractors. Yet suffering remains and is part of the mystery of our life in this world, and it is not only the unjust who suffer; in fact, they seem to suffer the least.

I believe that this world is a school, a character-building academy in the sacred art of loving, the art of caring for others. We are not in a position to make a definitive judgment about how others are learning and growing. Our task is to focus first on our own learning, and then to share, if we can, any wisdom we have gained. That is my purpose in writing. It's not that I am inherently wiser than anyone else. I have had the benefit of many years of schooling, including some experiences and awakenings not granted to everyone. I have been close to the suffering of many people, and also to their joys. If one hangs around long enough, and pays some attention, wisdom does come. Some of that wisdom, for me, is about gay, lesbian, bisexual, and transgender (referred to collectively by the acronym GLBT) persons. "Bisexual" refers to persons who can be sexually and affectionately attracted to persons of either sex. "Transgender" refers to persons whose inner sense of gender identity is at odds with the outward, biological characteristics of their sex. For them, a sex "change" in the eyes of the world is a coming home.

Let me conclude this letter with my view of what lies beyond; that is, where our schooling in this world is leading us—to a life in union with the source of all life, or toward a rejection of the Good News and its source. In other words, here is my view of heaven and hell.

This world, which places us on a bumpy ride alongside a variety of prickly persons, is preparing us for life in perfect community: for a realm where all gifts are freely offered and graciously received, and where fear does not exist. From birth onward, we are learning both to embrace and to let go of gifts. It's not easy to do either, whether we are facing what is new and strange or learning to hold less tightly to what is comfortable and familiar. The Good News gives us courage to believe in ourselves and our creator, and challenges us at every turn to be honest and courageous. It does not encourage us to pretend to be that which we are not or to deny the possibility that we may become more than we have been and find a larger Truth than we have yet seen.

The most important thing to believe about God is that God is *at least* as loving as we are. So any view of God that diminishes God's sense of compassion for all to less than we feel for our loved ones is insulting and unworthy of belief. I believe that, although the matter is finally in God's hands, heaven and hell are not assigned but chosen. We choose every day, in our decisions to love or not to love. A loving God will not compel us to live in a community where we would be miserable. We are free to opt out of heaven—if we prefer the alternatives, which are the prison of self or oblivion. In this life, at least, we always have the possibility of changing our minds. It may be that such freedom is extended into the next life as well. Our only fear should be of becoming persons too cold and shriveled to open to the light and warmth of God's love. We should fear God only in the sense of having reverential awe toward the one who is the source of our life at all times, and who knows us better than we know ourselves. We should never be afraid to reach out to God, no matter how we have failed or how unwisely we have chosen. God's grace reigns over all, even over our fears.

Fear is the enemy of love and growth. Fear makes us do terrible things to strangers, friends, and ourselves. It takes time to build trust between people, and much more time before we come to trust God enough to commit to God's purposes by giving ourselves freely in love. Faith in God is not a matter of what we think we are required to believe in order to be acceptable to God—such a perversion of obedience is a mockery of faith. Faith in God means putting our life deliberately into God's hands, in small and large things. Willingness to do so is the education of a lifetime and beyond.

To love God in spirit and truth means that we embrace God's purposes and, in reliance upon God, learn to love our neighbors— even those who don't strike us as particularly lovable. In the process of committing ourselves in this way we learn more about God, more about ourselves, and a lot more about our neighbors.

We come to see the virtues in others over time, even as we discover their weaknesses. To love someone is to come to respect that person's character and potential, and to make allowance for that person's flaws. However, that is not where love begins. We love because we have been loved—and not necessarily by the person to whom we are now reaching out. We love because love has become important to us, and it's too good to keep to ourselves. As we reach out in love, we learn what helps and doesn't help others to feel loved. The ideal in our minds of what it means to be loving has to be reshaped into a gift that another is glad to receive. So the Good News has to be told again and again, in the language of a new day, and has to be demonstrated in ways that make it credible to another.

It is a privilege to be ambassadors of the Good News, to be taken into God's confidence in this way. We have a sacred responsibility not to abuse the privilege or to diminish the life-giving power of the message. It is the Church corporately—all of its members—that is the "royal priesthood" (1 Pet. 2:9) acting as intermediary for the divine. In today's corporate terms, we all have a management responsibility to see that our church is expressing is the best and truest representation that we can share of what God offers to the world. Let us, then, be about the business of living God's reconciling love.

Yours in the great adventure . . .

Letter 2

Identifying the Core
of Our Common Faith

Dear Christian Believer:

You're still with me! I'm grateful. As I hope you may recognize, I'm writing to you as a fellow believer, one who has been touched by the Good News.

Because the Church has become so fragmented in regard to the details of Christian belief, I think we need to identify what is at the core of our common faith, rather than quibble about matters at the periphery. Let us aim for the bull's-eye if we can and allow for some variance in beliefs that are less central.

It seems to me that the proper center for our faith is no less than the person of Jesus. I hope that most Christians can agree on that. As Rowan Williams, the Archbishop of Canterbury, wrote in his 2003 Christmas letter to the Anglican Communion, "All human life finds its center and its goal in Jesus." Yet Jesus, even from his birth, was pushed to the margins during his lifetime.

Jesus remains a troubling presence in our world, because he represents divine purposes that exceed our understanding, and he calls us to change. The Archbishop wrote:

> No wonder that we push Jesus to the edge and try to avoid the implication of what he says and does. Yet we can't get away. . . . His will, his presence, his personal being is indeed what we most deeply want.

doi:10.1300/5661_02

He followed this with a startling assertion: "So *what looks like the edge is really the center.* Jesus is both a frightening stranger and the one who speaks to us with more intimacy and immediacy than any other being."

I think Rowan Williams has given utterance to a phrase that, like "God in a bottle," needs to reverberate in our consciousness as we venture to interpret and live the Good News in our tempestuous world. If Christians generally acknowledge that we may meet Christ in our neighbor, then it is not just the neighbor most familiar or congenial to us who may show us the center, but the one whose marginality exposes most dramatically where we remain unloving.

An urgent question, then, is the one posed on the bracelet that some Christians have worn, with the letters WWJD: "What Would Jesus Do?" In order to give an answer, and to describe the core or bull's-eye of our faith, we need to immerse ourselves in the Gospels, where we have four tapestries of what Jesus did. We need to enter, as fully as we can, into an awareness of how Jesus related to his neighbors: the powerful and the powerless, the esteemed and the despised. What attitudes did he encounter, and how did he respond? Where did he feel most strongly that people were missing the bull's-eye? For whom did he become an advocate? What needs did he identify? I cannot be exhaustive here, but will suggest an outline of an answer to these questions.

It is very tempting for us, while seeking to have a relationship with Jesus today, to make him "one of us," which means in most cases to see him as a middle-class American, sharing our cultural assumptions and antipathies. Surely Jesus would denounce the things that make us uncomfortable, would he not? Surely he would not call us to go out to the periphery of decent society in order to meet him—would he?

What did Jesus do and say? We will look at a representative sample from each of the four Gospels, starting with Mark, the shortest and very likely the earliest Gospel.

In the second chapter of Mark, conflict develops quickly. After his baptism by John and a retreat to the wilderness for a testing of his call, Jesus begins his public ministry and immediately begins to encounter criticism. He eats with sinners. His disciples do not fast, as do the Pharisees and the disciples of John. The disciples of Jesus pick grain on the Sabbath, to satisfy their hunger. Is Jesus lax in his standards of religious observance, or is another principle at work? The responses of Jesus to his critics suggest that his priorities are different from theirs, as follows: (1) it is more important and more practical to go to those who know they need help, than to those who think they are doing just fine; (2) it is more important to celebrate the presence of one who bears Good News than to observe the traditional niceties; and (3) religious observance is not an end in itself, but needs to serve God's mission to humankind. All of this is found in the second chapter of Mark.

As an illustration of how appearance often gets elevated above substance in the Church, I submit the following. When I was serving my first congregation in a small community in Nebraska, I was sitting in the bathtub when I got a phone call from one of the self-appointed patriarchs. It seems that he had been driving by the church earlier in the evening and saw me among those carrying clothes into the church for the rummage sale. As he thought about it later, it bothered him enough that he had to call me and chide me for doing that kind of undignified work in public view. Was his concern for me or for the image of the church he attended, as it reflected on him? As I stood some distance from my warm bath, dripping and listening to him, the absurdity of the scene was not lost on me. Which is more important—maintaining professional dignity or getting the work done?

Jesus encounters more opposition (Mark 3) when he performs a healing on the Sabbath. His response is to look on his accusers with anger and sadness at their "hardness of heart." He refutes the charge that he uses demonic power to cast out demons and suggests that to slander the Holy Spirit as they have done is a blasphemy against God. Finally, he makes it clear that his human family is not limited to blood relationships but includes all those who share a commitment to his mission.

In parables (Mark 4), Jesus teaches about the kingdom of God, which is becoming visible in his work. The kingdom grows, he says, in those who are prepared to receive it and who make it a priority. The kingdom is a truth that will one day be revealed to all.

The kingdom has a life of its own, and from small beginnings spreads out to provide blessings for many. The disciples see signs of the divine authority Jesus exercises, but they do not yet comprehend who he is.

Except in his hometown (Mark 6), where people know him too well to see any new possibilities, the reputation of Jesus is growing, but so is the opposition. Pharisees from Jerusalem come to observe his activities, and they note that he and his disciples are not fulfilling the traditional requirements of ritual cleanliness that they equate with dedication to God. Jesus replies tartly,

> Isaiah prophesied rightly about you hypocrites, as it is written, "This people honors me with their lips, but their hearts are far from me; in vain do they worship me, teaching human precepts as doctrines." You abandon the commandment of God and hold to human tradition. (Mark 7:6-8; quoting Isa. 29:13)

Jesus gathers the crowd around him and offers a teaching that follows from Isaiah. "Listen to me, all of you, and understand: there is nothing outside a person that by going in can defile, but the things that come out are what defile" (Mark 7:14-15). He adds, "For it is from within, from the human heart, that evil intentions come: fornication, theft, murder, adultery, avarice, wickedness, deceit, licentiousness, envy, slander, pride, folly. All these evil things come from within, and they defile a person" (Mark 7:21-23). This teaching challenges the popular notion today, which originated in Greek thought, that spiritual things are inward and are corrupted by outward or material things. What Jesus says is just the reverse: It is sin originating in the heart that corrupts the physical world.

What we have seen so far of the teaching and practice of Jesus suggests that he is less concerned with pious behavior than with caring for people in their need and less disturbed by violations of traditional practice than by someone's inability to love and trust and discern what is truly important.

As the Gospel of Mark continues to unfold, Jesus begins to prepare his disciples for his death and teaches that they must lay down their own lives in service. How different is this emphasis on self-giving from the self-serving consumer mentality so prevalent in American churches today, where the concern so often seems to be:

How can *I* get what *I* want from God and from church?
How can *I* feel secure?
How can *I* remain free from sin, so that *I* am acceptable to God?
How can *I* be sure that *I* am going to heaven?

It is the difference between a leap of faith and having "God in a bottle."

In the Gospel according to Luke, we find some striking instances of God's self-giving portrayed in human examples. A woman described only as "a sinner" approaches Jesus while he is at table in a Pharisee's house and proceeds to weep at his feet, then to kiss and anoint his feet. Far from being offended by this intrusion, Jesus uses the occasion to teach his host about the primacy of love over social or religious propriety. This woman has shown faith and love. "Therefore," says Jesus, "her sins, which were many, have been forgiven; hence she has shown great love. But the one to whom little is forgiven, loves little" (Luke 7:47). In other words, God pours out love generously to those who in their need and vulnerability are able to receive it. In contrast, those who rest secure in their presumed sinlessness before God, like the host in this account, neither give much nor receive much.

Jesus encounters a lawyer who asks, "What must I do to inherit eternal life?" (Luke 10:25). The lawyer knows what God requires in general—love God and love your neighbor—but he presses to determine the limits of his obligation, asking Jesus, "Who is my neighbor?" (Luke 10:29). Jesus responds with the parable of the Good Samaritan, which is often taken simply to show how far we should go in loving our neighbor: go beyond what is required, and care even for those who see themselves as superior to you. However, Jesus adds a twist in the way he frames the moral to answer the lawyer's question, asking him: "Which of these three [the two respectable religious people who passed by, or the not-so-respectable outsider who stopped to help], do you think was a neighbor to the man who fell into the hands of the robbers?" (Luke 10:36). When the lawyer answers correctly, "The one who showed mercy," Jesus says, "Go and do likewise" (Luke 10:37). The question for me, as Jesus posed it to the lawyer, is not just "Whom should *I* help?" but "Who helps me when *I* am in trouble?"

Somewhere around 1985 I borrowed an old recreational vehicle from a parishioner and took my family on a vacation to Texas. We dodged a hurricane, drove through all the major cities in Texas in this twenty-eight-foot behemoth, and made it most of the way home without incident. Then, on a lonely road in northern Kansas, a valve stuck in the fuel line as I was switching from one gas tank to the other, and we were stalled, stranded, helpless. Who came along and gave me a ride into town to get help? Not another family like ours. No, it was a Native American—a person who I daresay was not used to getting a great deal of respect from white, middle-class families. That day he was the Samaritan on the road.

Who is going to help you when you are in need? It may not be the person you expect. However, very likely God will send someone, and someday you will be the person God sends to help someone who will be rather surprised to see *you.*

The custodians of traditional piety complain that "This fellow welcomes sinners and eats with them" (Luke 15:2). Jesus responds by telling a series of parables about God seeking the lost, capped by the parable of the prodigal son. The three characters in the story are the irresponsible, but later repentant younger brother; the responsible but resentful and unforgiving older brother; and the patient, generous, forgiving father. I would venture to say that if our lives are viewed as an extended drama, we have played all three roles in the story. We have been the glad recipients of "grace," which means love freely given, undeserved, often extravagant; we have been the ones judgmental and aloof, unwilling to enter into a celebration for the homecoming of one who clearly doesn't deserve it; and we, especially if we have been parents, have been the extenders of grace, motivated by love overriding all concern that we might be "rewarding misbehavior" (as the respon-

sible brother would say) or failing to teach a lesson to the one leaning toward irresponsibility.

A popular view of the Church is that its primary role must be
upholder of public morality, and the Bible is primarily viewed as a
book of God's laws to govern human behavior. However, when we
read these Gospel stories just cited, a different view emerges: of
the Church as a community of grace, and of the Bible as a mirror
of God's generous love, flowing especially through the person and
work of Jesus.

When we move from Luke to the Gospel according to Matthew,
the Sermon on the Mount (Chapters 5 through 7) is a notable fea-
ture. Again and again in this extended series of pronouncements,
Jesus raises the bar from doing what the law requires to going beyond what is required, giving oneself fully. The demand or call of
God expressed here must be dismaying to anyone who is asking,
as was the lawyer in Luke, "How far do I need to go in order to satisfy God?" Jesus says, "Unless your righteousness exceeds that of
the scribes and Pharisees [the most zealous upholders of the law],
you will never enter the kingdom of heaven" (Matt. 5:20). Even
more shocking, he says, "Be perfect, therefore, as your heavenly
Father is perfect" (Matt. 5:48). What is going on here? How can
we even attempt to play such a losing game? Yet Jesus does not
leave us without hope. We are invited, as in the Lord's Prayer
(Matt. 6:9-13), to ask God for whatever we need, we are encouraged not to be anxious about our physical needs (Matt. 6:25-33),
and we are promised that we will find whatever we seek (Matt.
7:8). Jesus sets forth two principles to govern our thinking—one
about the character of God, and one about our approach to our
neighbor. With regard to God's disposition toward us, Jesus says,
"If you then, who are evil, know how to give good gifts to your
children, how much more will your Father in heaven give good
things to those who ask him!" (Matt. 7:11). Immediately thereaf-
ter he sets forth the golden rule to govern our stance toward our
neighbor: "In everything do to others as you would have them do
to you; for this is the law and the prophets" (Matt. 7:12).

The overall effect of the Sermon on the Mount, I submit, is to
bring us to our knees in prayer and humble dependence upon God.

Can we be perfect as our heavenly Father is perfect? Certainly not, at least not with our own strength. Jesus invites us to abandon our reliance upon justifying ourselves before God and put our lives into God's hands for mercy and empowerment. The implication that can hardly be avoided is this: Just as we are radically dependent upon God's grace, in order to be pleasing to God, so we must abandon our presumption of judging others. Jesus says explicitly (Matt. 7:1-2), "Do not judge, so that you may not be judged. For with the judgment you make you will be judged, and the measure you give will be the measure you get back." The human tendency, says Jesus in the next verse, is to notice the speck in our neighbor's eye while overlooking the log in our own. We are invited to liberate others and ourselves from that kind of nonsense, and to discover a love that is greater than judgment, a love that is generous to all.

Finally, in the Gospel according to John, Jesus sums up his message and prepares his disciples for their ministry in an extended teaching at the Last Supper (Chapters 13-17). What he teaches them, beginning with the foot washing and culminating in his prayer for the unity of the Church, is that they are to follow his lead. He says, "I give you a new commandment, that you love one another" (John 13:34, reiterated in John 15:12). If there is a core to the message of Jesus, this is clearly it for John.

All four Gospels, therefore, witness to the teaching and action of Jesus setting forth the way of self-giving love as the way of the kingdom of God, as in this exchange between Jesus and Philip: "Have I been with you all this time, Philip, and you still do not know me? Whoever has seen me has seen the Father" (John 14:9). The message is love in action, not a code of belief. The standard of judgment is not a code of law but an openness to give and receive grace. The authority of Jesus is the authority of one who models what he or she preaches, showing forth the reign of God in the new life he or she graciously bestows.

In the Epistles of Paul, likewise, the core of faith focuses on the person of Jesus and on the free gift of God's love as the basis for our response of love and discipleship. Four letters of Paul, which appear back to back, make a point of how easily the Gospel can be corrupted, so that the Good News is lost, when Christians become preoccupied with how things look and with getting the neighbor to shape up. Let's take these examples one by one.

In Galatians 2, Paul refers to an incident when he had to rebuke Peter, the first great preacher of the Gospel, when Peter lost his nerve and reverted to the Jewish custom of not having table fellowship with Gentiles, for fear of criticism. Paul then reiterates the basis of his faith, as one who has been pronounced acceptable through faith in Christ, rather than by observing the law. He says, "I do not nullify the grace of God; for if justification comes through the law, then Christ died for nothing" (Gal. 2:21). He emphasizes the point again in Chapter 5: "For freedom Christ has set us free. Stand firm, therefore, and do not submit again to a yoke of slavery" (Gal. 5:1).

Paul's challenge comes ringing down to our own day, when there are plenty of Christians willing to take away our God-given freedom and tell us what we should and shouldn't do, whether in our political actions, in the company we keep, in our sex lives, or in our recreational pursuits. Paul challenges us to have the courage of our convictions, in making our own decisions about what does or doesn't honor God, and in allowing our neighbors to exercise their freedom, as well.

It's not that Paul is saying that what I do doesn't matter. He respects what God is doing in me: setting me free, changing my heart, making me a practitioner of love. I have the great honor and responsibility of making choices as an agent of God's love. I am now a member of God's family, not a slave in God's household. I may choose to refrain from exercising my freedom so as not to injure others (cf. 1 Cor. 8). However, my freedom is now *for* something: It is given so that I may grow and glorify God, and one way I grow is by making mistakes.

I was filled with a mixture of pride and dread when each one of my children was issued a driver's license. It was a sign of growing up, but also a new exposure to harm and liability. Despite our best efforts to prepare them, new drivers are going to make some mistakes and sooner or later—generally sooner—have an accident. It proved to be that way with my kids, just as I had to learn the hard way in my own education as a driver. We can only pray that the first accident, when it comes, will not be too serious, and that the needed lessons will be learned. I did not hold my kids back from driving because I was afraid. I knew that love and not fear had to be my overriding principle. I wanted my kids to grow and become self-governing.

In Ephesians, the formula is stated: "By grace you have been saved through faith, and this is not your own doing; it is the gift of God—not the result of works, so that no one may boast" (Eph. 2:8-9). Paul goes on, as he did in Galatians, to urge us to make good use of this gift of acceptance and freedom, so that others may find their own freedom and dignity in relationship to God.

We are set free not just from condemnation, but also from slavery to false gods. Thus, we are urged to "live as children of light" (Eph. 5:8). Paul is not at all reluctant to suggest what we ought to avoid, but he does not, in so doing, revoke the Good News. He simply wants us to cherish and make the best use of the freedom we have been given.

In Philippians, Paul holds up the example of Jesus, "who, though he was in the form of God, did not regard equality with God as something to be exploited, but emptied himself, taking the form of a slave, being born in human likeness" (Phil. 2:6-7)—ultimately giving himself up to death. Following this example, Paul urges: "Work out your own salvation with fear and trembling, for it is God who is at work in you . . ." (Phil. 2:12-13). In other words, exercising my freedom is a sobering responsibility, but God is with me in the enterprise, helping me to grow in learning and serving the purposes of love.

Paul contrasts his life before he became centered in Jesus with the life he now lives as a disciple and apostle. He had been a Pharisee, and a good one. However, now his basis of approval has changed, and he writes:

> Whatever gains I had, these I have come to regard as loss because of Christ. . . . For his sake I have suffered the loss of all things, and I regard them as rubbish, in order that I may gain

Christ and be found in him, not having a righteousness of my own. . . . (Phil. 3:7-9)

Can you hear the strength of those words? Rule-bound standing with God is seen as "rubbish"—garbage—in comparison to the supreme value of being in the flow of God's love in Christ. Paul laments the folly of those who refuse to center their lives in the love of Jesus, who settle instead for false gods. No doubt he is ruefully recalling how his own attempts to serve the one true God became perverted by his obsession with observance of rules and judgment of others, but his own mind and heart are now living in the goodness of what God has freely given to him in Christ: a new beginning, a new chance to serve God and live life to its fullest potential; not in grasping but in serving, as Jesus did.

Finally, in Colossians, Paul once again centers his teaching in the person of Jesus ("He is the image of the invisible God. . . ." Col. 1:15) and urges others to "put on love" as their clothing (Col. 3:14) and to "let the peace of Christ rule in your hearts" (Col. 3:15). Again he warns against those who will subvert the Good News by adding requirements that are human and not divine. "See to it that no one takes you captive through philosophy and empty deceit, according to human tradition. . . ." (Col. 2:8). "Do not let anyone condemn you in matters of food and drink or of observing festivals, new moons or sabbaths. These are only a shadow of what is to come, but the substance belongs to Christ" (Col. 2:16-17). He pleads:

> If with Christ you died to the elemental spirits of the universe, why do you still live as if you belonged to the world? Why do you submit to regulations, "Do not handle, do not taste, do not touch?" All these regulations refer to things that perish with use; they are simply human commands and teachings. (Col. 2:20-22)

The false gods of our day are both religious and nonreligious. They are the gods of this culture, which has a patina of Christianity but at heart displays a value system that worships money and power, status and success, and security and control, paying only lip-service to caring for people and walking in the way of the cross.

The Gospel as set forth by Jesus and Paul is corrupted when church leaders—people who presume to speak for God—use the word of God, not to liberate people for the cause of love but to re-enslave them in the interests of serving the contemporary church and culture. Ironically and blasphemously, these church leaders accuse the more liberal denominations of "selling out to the culture," when it is they who have sold out to the comforts of what Robert Bellah, in his contributions to the book *Habits of the Heart: Individualism and Commitment in American Life,* has called "enclave thinking" (cf. p. 154) in contemporary America: gathering a group of the like-minded and walling out anyone whose views or needs would challenge that group's assumptions about morality and faithfulness to Christ.

The Good News of Jesus Christ is love overcoming fear; it is not putting "the fear of God" into people so that they can be more easily controlled. Time and again the New Testament affirms that Jesus spoke with authority. His authority was the authority of truth lived as well as proclaimed: an openness to the stranger, a willingness to go the extra mile, and even a willingness to sacrifice himself. He often spoke in a confrontational way, but left his hearers free to make their own choices, honoring their dignity as moral agents. He preached a kingdom open to all, a kingdom built upon the power of love, not the love of power.

The opposition that Jesus encountered was mostly from people heavily invested in the status quo, people who were getting along just fine following the existing rules and power relationships. What grieved Jesus most was the spiritual blindness and lack of love he encountered, the inability of so many to put themselves into the place of an outsider or of someone who had failed and was seeking to make a new beginning. He did not go out of his way to avoid those on the margins of society, but welcomed them and took their hungers seriously. He identified sin not so much in terms of outward observance, but as selfishness and smallness of spirit originating in the heart.

Jesus did not live in personal isolation, even when the world rejected him. In prayer he relied on his divine family: the Father who loved him, and the Holy Spirit who empowered him to heal and impart wisdom. He saw the whole world potentially as his family, forgiving even those who put him to death. His faith was not a matter of walling out those who disagreed with him, but of living the truth shown to him by the spirit.

When I see what Jesus did according to the biblical record, and how he changed the life of a Pharisee such as Paul, it saddens me to see Jesus misrepresented as an enforcer of contemporary prejudice or one who condemns and excludes instead of welcoming the honest seeker. Churches are always in danger of becoming the new home for Pharisees in our own day. In the next letter I will have more to say about the nature of sin and what love requires. Until then, I am . . .

Yours in Jesus,

Letter 3

What Gets in the Way of Love

Dear Learner in Love:

Thanks for hanging in there with me, as we go deeper into the Good News and its applications. As Paul believed in his Epistles, I'm trusting that what has convinced and blessed me may have a similar impact on you.

What is love, and what is sin? It has been said that love, like beauty, "is in the eye of the beholder." However, I would suggest that love is much more than what I like or what makes me happy. Love is God-stuff, integral to the purposes and processes of creation. Evil is whatever opposes those purposes and processes.

In the Book of Common Prayer 1979, the Presentation and Examination of the Candidates in the service of Holy Baptism has three questions about resisting evil, in effect sorting evil into three categories: cosmic, institutional or worldly, and personal.

> *Cosmic evil:* "Do you renounce Satan and all the spiritual forces of wickedness that rebel against God?"
> *Institutional evil:* "Do you renounce the evil powers of this world which corrupt and destroy the creatures of God?"
> *Personal evil, that is, sin:* "Do you renounce all sinful desires that draw you from the love of God?"

Love has both intentional and unintentional enemies; that is, not everyone who is opposing love does so in full awareness. However, even awareness may be partly a choice. In his second book, *People of the Lie,* M. Scott Peck (1983) showed in accounts from

doi:10.1300/5661_03

his clinical practice of psychiatry that garden-variety evil amounts to an unwillingness to inconvenience oneself for the sake of another person, even if that person is one's own child, and even if that unwillingness inflicts great suffering upon the other. It is chilling to realize that some people in this world are not only quite undisturbed by the suffering of others—of that we are all guilty, to some degree—but also are unwilling even to consider the possibility of making a different choice, in order to spare another person great suffering.

We call gaps in personal awareness "blind spots," giving the benefit of the doubt to someone who is acting in an unloving way but doesn't know it. However, what happens when someone points out *my* blind spot? Do I accept such feedback humbly and even gratefully, or do I resist and deny such a reality check? Most of us are inclined to have hurt feelings and to protect our egos when our failures are exposed. The use of defense mechanisms is normal, to a degree. In Peck's view, such resistance becomes pathological when a person so exposed chooses to remain blind so as not to be inconvenienced. As a colleague recently pointed out in a sermon, "sin" has an "I" in the middle.

How do blind spots arise? They are part of our innate (or, as the Bible would say, fallen) human tendency to think of ourselves first and others later, perhaps *much* later. When I was first a student at Virginia Theological Seminary, A.T. Mollegen was Professor of New Testament. Dr. Mollegen was fond of saying: "Original sin means that if you are standing on my foot, I am more likely to know it than you are."

Let's take an everyday example. I go out to lunch with some friends, all of whom have significantly higher incomes than I do. We go to a nice restaurant, where the policy is not to provide separate checks. My friends all order a beverage; I do not. My entrée is a more modest one than the others are having. When the check comes, one of my friends quickly figures that, with tip, if everyone throws in $20, it will come out just right. That is about twice what I would have paid, had I gone solo. How do I feel about my friend's insensitive suggestion?

Now let's say I take my family of five out for a modest dinner, and I'm picking up the check. The tab, with tax, comes to $75. Our waitress has brought us refills on our drinks and has given us good service. She is middle-aged and obviously on her feet a lot. I have no idea what her base salary may be, apart from tips, or what financial responsibilities she carries. How much do I tip and why? Would it make a difference if I had worked as a waiter?

Injustice has an intense reality when I experience it myself. When it happens to someone else, it's a lot more abstract and easy to overlook or rationalize. The second great commandment according to Jesus (Mark 12:31) is, "You shall love your neighbor as yourself." That not only sums up commandments five through ten of the Ten Commandments but implicitly goes further: If I am going to love my neighbor, I will need to make an effort to learn what difficulties my neighbor is experiencing, since I am not as aware of that as I am of my own difficulties.

A related deficiency that must be addressed if I am going to love my neighbor as myself is the double standard. The classic double standard with which many of us are familiar has to do with the difference between how men and women are scrutinized with regard to their sexual behavior. Women still find themselves much more subject to critical scrutiny of their sexual habits, perhaps because the responsibility of pregnancy and child rearing falls more heavily upon them.

A double standard also exists in the way heterosexual couples and homosexual couples are judged in our society, whether they are casual or committed. Fornication, which means any sex outside of marriage, is listed as a sin by St. Paul, but it is winked at with regard to heterosexual couples, many if not most of whom cohabit prior to marriage or even engagement. Homosexuals, however, are seen by many as immoral unless they remain strictly celibate—permanently. This is particularly true of anyone who seeks to be an ordained leader in the Church, where there is also a double standard between church members and clergy, the latter being persons who are supposed to "set the example."

Double standards reveal a deficiency in loving; that is, a reluctance or unwillingness to imagine what it might be like to be on the other side of the double standard. Just as Caucasians are often oblivious to what is accurately termed "white privilege" and quick to deny the charge of racism, since we are mostly unaware of our complicity in such privilege, heterosexuals remain mostly blind to the unequal treatment we enjoy in society. Such blindness allows us to resist Christ's call to love, because we do not see where love is lacking.

I have suggested, dear reader, that sin is a resistance to God's call to love one's neighbor as oneself, but what does love really mean? Erich Fromm, C. S. Lewis, and others have identified some standard varieties of human love, each valuable and important in its own way.

One kind of affection and caring exists within families, whether one is a biological member or a member by adoption. Family members are often willing to make sacrifices for one another that they would be unlikely to make for someone outside the family. The flip side of this is that lines may be drawn, so that persons outside the family receive less consideration. At its best, to those who are inside the family circle, it is warm and cozy, a shelter of forgiveness and acceptance that allows children and adults to have a secure home base from which to venture into the world. At its worst, family love reinforces a view of the world that is "us versus them," hardly a model for loving one's neighbor as oneself.

Another variety of love is faithful friendship, either between persons of the same gender or across genders. Friendship is generally simpler and seen as more pure, if no sexual element is involved. The strength of friendship is that it affirms us and makes us feel less alone, less dependent on being part of a family or being in an exclusive sexual relationship. Friends help us to learn more about ourselves, our assets and liabilities. Friends stand by us in times of difficulty, as do family members. Friends may share an affinity of interests and personality with us, or they may be rather different and complementary. It is difficult to find a downside to friendship, except that it may compete with other relationships. Good marriages have a strong friendship at the core. Friendship endures, even during periods when passion is relatively cool.

Erotic love is the basis of romance, as well as of the perpetuation of the species. It is the attraction that gives enormous energy and creativity to life, even when the attraction cannot be consummated. Most sexual acts do not result in conception, yet may be highly enriching in terms of personal affirmation, bringing a bloom to one's cheeks and a spring to one's walk, and, in terms of intimacy, bringing a sense of deeply understanding—and being deeply understood by—another. Even when the sex act is not a possibility, the attraction itself has an energy that, like the completed act, can be blessing or curse, depending on how it is managed. Lust is listed as one of the seven deadly sins, not because erotic love is shameful but because its exercise can be abusive or addictive. At its best, erotic love is a celebration of the beauty and goodness of God's creation. At its worst, erotic love becomes a false god, leading persons to disappointment or destruction and diverting them from fulfillment in service to the one true God.

The highest kind of human love we know encompasses and transcends all the other varieties, because it flows in the main channel of the Holy Spirit. Paul describes this love (in Greek the word is *agape*) in 1 Corinthians 13. It is the selfless love that we see in instances of personal sacrifice—supremely in the passion and death of Jesus. What makes this self-giving love special is that it is focused entirely on helping the one who is loved to achieve and become more. Because this kind of generosity requires reserves of courage and caring that are more than human, we know that when we are seeing it we are seeing God in action.

Although all love finds its origin in God and reflects the goodness of God, agape brings us closest to the purposes and character of God. Faithfulness and caring are good; appreciation and comradeship are good; pleasure and longing for the beautiful are good; but only self-giving love has the power to transform us into the image of the God, in whose likeness we were created. The love of Jesus is the love that enables us to take up our crosses and follow him, forgiving those who treat us badly and valuing all people as children of God.

Some years ago a friend told me, "I cannot imagine that there is anything you could do that would make me stop loving you."

I really wanted to believe that, but I took that statement as a sincere and affectionate gesture, not a guarantee, because it came from a human being. In the long run, that promise failed to hold true. Nevertheless, it was a touching human expression of the unconditional love of God that is the essence of the Good News.

The love of God is the power that creates and maintains the universe at every moment. It is the power in prayer and in healing. When I intercede for someone, or lay my hands in prayer upon someone's head in quest of greater wholeness for them, I put myself intentionally into the stream of God's loving work, allowing God's power to flow more freely through me, blessing me as well as the other person.

All of us are learners in love, as was the character Bill Murray played in the movie *Groundhog Day,* trapped into repeating the same day over and over. At first he thought that it was a cruel joke, and then that his learning was merely a matter of refining his tactics, avoiding the pitfalls he had previously experienced. However, as his education continued, he changed as a person, becoming a member of the community because he truly cared, not just as a strategy. As his focus changed from grasping to giving, he found that he couldn't avoid being loved in return. In a profound way, he had to die to his own hopes in order to find the blessing God was preparing for him.

It would be tempting to impose the moral of *Groundhog Day* upon all the learners in love, encouraging them to make sacrifices in the service of God's will for their lives and evaluating their day-to-day progress in that quest. However, that would be a strategy of avoidance, an undercutting of the film's message and sly power. *Groundhog Day* is not a lesson for others; it is an invitation to me to accept the challenges and opportunities of my own captivity in this world.

When my father-in-law was dying of cancer, at what is my present age, I told him by letter that it was possible that he might find meaning in his suffering, but that it was a meaning only he could claim; no one else could assign it for him. In the same way, all of us have the possibility of finding God at work in the midst of our suffering, but we do not have the right to tell someone else, "Your suffering is secondary to the great thing God is doing in your life." I need to ask myself when I am so tempted: "Whose need for meaning and security is being met here?"

All of us have a hunger for love and a hunger to be part of something bigger than ourselves. Sometimes these hungers seem to be in conflict, as in the parable of the wedding banquet in Matthew 22. The banquet is open to all who are willing to attend; but there is one requirement: Every guest must wear the wedding garment, which is presumably provided by the host. Is this "dress code" an unreasonable requirement? Not if we catch the drift of the parable, which points us to the heavenly wedding banquet of Jesus and his bride, the Church. What is the garment required for all in attendance? It is to put on the love of the bridegroom, as in Colossians 3, the love that accepts all the others present. A conflict may arise in our hearts, however, because each of us would like to be acknowledged as special. We want to be loved without having to love all the others. Unfortunately, there can be no true love celebration unless everyone is on the same footing. If God is willing, even eager, to let me in, I have to be willing for others to be let in as well, including those of whom I did not previously approve. It is God's party, and I am one of many guests, not a solo bride. If that makes me feel less special, then I still have some learning in love to do.

Children may wish that their parents loved them more than their siblings, and may fear that just the opposite is true. Parents may show favoritism instead of valuing each child uniquely with equal devotion. It's understandable that we want to be special, because if we are, then we are indispensable. If we are just like all the others, then why should God, or our parents, or whoever loves us, be greatly concerned to keep us around?

In our age, the cult of celebrity is the secular manifestation of our desire to be special. People will endure amazing hardships and even humiliations in order to be on television and known to millions, quite apart from any other prize that might be awarded. Becoming a celebrity is a way of saying, "I was here; my life mattered." People have even committed murder to gain such attention, just as a child who can't seem to win parental notice by approved means will seek attention through misbehavior.

Evil has no life of its own; it creates nothing except destruction. Evil feeds upon goodness, upon life. Notice, dear friend, that evil is "l-i-v-e" backward. The attraction of evil is the distortion and perversion of something originally good. Evil is parasitic: it gives nothing, but drains the life out of that to which it attaches itself. Love, by contrast, builds up the person or thing to which it is attached.

What makes a good love story? Based on many years of reading and going to movies, I would say that a good love story, along with having characters who seem real because they are flawed, combines the following elements: Someone risks or pays a price in the cause of love, someone changes for the better, and the right people get together. Sometimes the change comes too late for them to get together, and the story still has power. If nothing is truly ventured, nothing is truly won—not in the story, not for us.

My favorite movie of all time is *An Officer and a Gentleman*. After I first saw it, when I came out of the theater, I couldn't talk about it casually; I felt I was walking on holy ground. As I thought about it more later, it struck me that all the major varieties of love are present in this movie: the friendship between Zack (played by Richard Gere) and his fellow trainee Sid (played by David Keith); the romantic relationship between Zack and Paula (played by Debra Winger), which also has a strong element of friendship; and the "father love" of Sergeant Foley (played by Lou Gossett Jr.), who comes to care for Zack as a son.

In the movie, Zack Mayo is a loner who has learned to depend on no one, because his mother died when he was young and his father mostly neglected him. Zack learned to protect himself, physically and emotionally. His friendship with Sid begins to soften his shell, creating the illusion, at least, of belonging to a community. However, this development cannot really emerge until Zack deals with Sergeant Foley, who tells all the candidates that, if they want to become Navy pilots, they have to get by him.

The pivotal event in the movie takes place on a weekend, when Sergeant Foley isolates Zack and tries to break down his resistance.

Why is Zack such a lone wolf, so averse to being a team player? Sergeant Foley is determined either to get inside Zack's head or to force him out of the program, but when he finally gets Zack to the breaking point, two amazing things happen. The first is that Zack begs him not to force him out: "Don't you do that!"—in the next breath confessing, "I got nowhere else to go!" In that moment of pain and vulnerability, Sergeant Foley sees into Zack's soul. Then the second amazing thing happens: Sergeant Foley steps over the line, from prosecutor to advocate. It is the most moving thing I have ever seen in cinema.

Zack and Sergeant Foley are not quite through challenging each other, but from that weekend on, Zack is in some respects a changed man—more humble, more generous, ready to be a team player. He is still guarding the door of his heart, however.

Another great moment in the film takes place in the aftermath of the graduation of the new officers. Zack looks around as hats are tossed into the air, and sees that, unlike the others, he is alone. He also realizes, soon enough, that he doesn't have to be. Another person has shown herself to be true—Paula. Like her friend Lynette, Paula had initially seen marriage to "an officer and a gentleman" as instant status and an escape from her depressing working-class life. Unlike Lynette, who was not prepared to lose her prize and so trapped Sid into marriage with a false pregnancy, Paula declares her love with no strings attached. When Sid's tragic death by suicide confirms Zack's fear of being attached to anyone, Paula absorbs Zack's anger without lashing back. At the end of the film, her honesty and caring are rewarded.

Both Sergeant Foley and Paula are human in their seeking to be successful, but they prove capable of reaching beyond their own concerns. What I see operating in their willingness to suffer for the sake of caring is that most excellent self-giving love that is more than human. That was the holy ground I experienced and to which I responded, though I could not at first name it.

Love stories can teach us that we don't have to relive the same day over and over; we can learn through the real or imagined lives of others. I hope, dear reader, that you appreciate love stories too. If so, I think you will appreciate some stories I have yet to tell.

I hope that you have appreciated many of the stories in the Bible, which is itself a kind of love story written by two communities: the community of Israel and the community of the Church. In my next letter, I will write about that latter community, of which many of us are a part.

Yours in the School of Love,

Letter 4

Recognizing the Church
As Both Human and Divine

Dear Church Lover:

It's not easy to do much of the time, is it? To love the Church. The Church can be so exasperating, much like living in any large, unruly family. Yet you and I—and that weird guy over there—and that gal who thinks she's better than both of us—all together, we are the Body of Christ. Amazing! What was God thinking?

The Church is not only the keeper of the sacraments—in catholic tradition, those "outward and visible signs of an inward and spiritual grace"; she is herself a sacrament, that is, an extension of the life of Jesus, the incarnation of God in this world. As such, the Church is both human and divine—visibly human, not so visibly divine.

The thing about sacraments is that there is always more to them than meets the eye. Let's consider two examples, one inside the Church and one outside.

We baptize a baby, not because the baby is ready to believe and commit to the faith of the Church, but because those who love the baby want to bring that child into the nurturing fellowship of the Church. At least, we hope that's what they are doing, and not just ensuring their child's future beyond this life. In the baptismal service in the Book of Common Prayer 1979, the congregation present at the baptism is asked this question: "Will you who witness these vows do all in your power to support this child in her life in Christ?" Of course, the church members present declare, "We

doi:10.1300/5661_04

will." They can only fulfill this vow, however, with the cooperation of the parents and other adults who take a close personal interest in the developing child. One other player must be considered, though, not counting the child. That is God, who is also present at the baptism and ready to go to work. We cannot see God's work in our lives directly, only as we see the effects, and then generally in hindsight, but a drama is going on under the surface of this little girl's life, and witnesses are surrounding her and lifting her up in a vast assembly of love and prayer. These witnesses are the Communion of Saints, that is, all those present or departed who are members of the Mystical Body of Christ, the Church not divided by boundaries of space and time.

When a child is baptized, water is used as the outward sign of conveying the gift of new life in the family of God. What are some components of that gift? These include incorporation into the Body of Christ, both now and in the life to come; forgiveness of sins, making our continuing fellowship with God possible; the gift of the Holy Spirit, for life and growth in community; and the right and responsibility of meaningful service as a member of the Body. Ministry is a calling into which we grow as we come to greater awareness of the gifts we have received. It is a manifestation of God working in our life, enabling us to glimpse the majestic purpose of the One who has brought us into the family.

Here is a more everyday example, which at first may appear to have nothing to do with the Church. Two friends, Larry and Bill, get together for lunch every Wednesday. It has become a ritual for them, after many months. What goes on at their lunch? To watch them, you might think, "Nothing much." They order from the menu, joke around, share current news. Those are the outward and visible signs. However, underneath the ritual, some deeper things are happening: the friendship is being reaffirmed; a commitment of fidelity, more than mere habit, is being observed; and the message is being communicated at various levels: "I care about you. You are a person worth caring about. I want you in my life." These luncheons are not a formal sacrament, but they have a sacramental character. In a real way, they are part of the Church in action outside the walls.

The Catechism of the Book of Common Prayer 1979 enumerates four "marks" of the Church: the Church is one, holy, catholic, and apostolic. What does each of these marks mean, and why should we care? Each of these can be seen in a positive way, as a sign of God's involvement in the Church, and also in contrast to movements masquerading as Church.

I'm beginning with the second of these marks—the Church is holy—because that takes me back to the beginning of my ordained ministry, when I was called to serve a small church in a small town in central Nebraska. When I first arrived, an elderly member named Frank took one look at me and was heard to blurt out, quite in keeping with his name: "Why, he's just a boy!" The doubts were not strictly one-way. As I served that congregation for a while, rising to the pastoral challenges—and there were many—I came to ask myself: "How does this congregation survive?" I went down the list of members, and it seemed to me that nearly everyone was on shaky ground: either in poor health, or in a shaky marriage, or struggling with a major problem such as addiction. The answer that came to me was: this congregation survives only because God is committed to it. That was years before I had heard of Julian of Norwich, who was shown by God that the whole creation in God's care is like a hazelnut in the palm of one's hand: it endures not because of its size, but because it is loved. For all its shakiness, that congregation was a dwelling place of the Holy Spirit. Clergy had come and gone, and more would come and go after I left, yet the congregation stubbornly endured. The Church is holy, not because its members display marks of great spiritual effectiveness, but because, for all its faults, the Church has not been deserted by God.

The real issue in thinking about the presence or absence of the Holy Spirit in any individual congregation or denomination, it seems to me, is not the style of worship or whether one is used to thinking about sacraments but how the Holy Spirit is perceived to work in the life of a believer and in relationship to holy scripture. Is the Holy Spirit a form of magic, or is it organic to one's living as a Christian in this world? Is the spirit simply a witness to the power and truth of the word of God, or is it the spirit that enlivens the word and makes it a contemporary utterance to us from the

Lord? At my second stop in ordained ministry I had a chance to explore these questions.

After three and a half years in my first charge I was drafted as a utility player in the big leagues, called to serve on staff of the mother church of Kalamazoo, Michigan, a large downtown parish headed by a sage veteran priest. How could anyone resist a call to the other end of the road from Timbuktu? However, I found that all the action in Kalamazoo was not inside the parish. Soon after my arrival, I was drawn into contact with various segments of the charismatic movement, a stream of renewal with both Catholic and Protestant roots.

I learned that there were immature and mature charismatics, and the difference between them was the difference between night and day: the difference between pretension and genuine ministry in the spirit. The immature charismatics I saw were preoccupied with speaking in tongues as the sign that they had "got it" and with the quest for the perfect church and the next experiential high. They measured a church's openness to the spirit by the style of music, the informality of the liturgy, and by how many people were willing to put their hands into the air as an expression of rapturous praise. Mature charismatics, on the other hand, accepted moments of intensity but were also able to operate in a lower key, with love as their central principle, focusing on the needs of others and what would build up the Church in unity.

The Church is One. What I found in Kalamazoo was a series of encounters with unity in diversity: the Holy Spirit at work in visible and surprising ways. I discovered this process, for example, in a class I taught for two years, preparing teachers to lead adult Bible study. The members of that class differed from one another in personality, education, and style of religiosity; yet these differences proved to be an enrichment rather than an impediment to the communal life we developed. I saw in that class of eleven disciples the potential in the body of Christ. The same held true for other groups that I facilitated: Marriage Encounter fellowship, youth group, and our self-designed Sunday school. In each case a significant ministry emerged from a collection of people that was by no means homogeneous.

The Church today is experiencing a test of its ability to accommodate people with a wide range of convictions. Diversity is good, but prolonged controversy may not be so good. People weary of conflict within a group often leave just to relieve the tension, quite apart from their particular opinions.

The Church's unity has never been a matter of silencing all disagreement or consorting only with the like-minded. When Jesus prayed "that they may all be one" (John 17:21), he was seeking not a consensus on doctrine, but a unity of relationship, inward and outward. The unity for which he prayed is based on the centrality of the love that casts out fear and calls us to a common purpose. Could Jesus have envisioned the proliferation of denominations we have today? Does such proliferation mean we should now disregard his prayer?

Throughout my ordained ministry I have heard lip service paid to the principle that the Church is One, but I have seen relatively little time and energy invested in living out that unity through ecumenical cooperation. The word "ecumenical," which comes from the Greek word meaning house or household, implies that all churches are part of the same household, all in the same boat navigating the stormy seas en route to the destination God has prepared for us. To what degree does that vision animate my ministry? I am keenly aware of the differences that separate our denominations. How much effort am I willing to expend to discover and build upon what we have in common? So much needs to be done within the typical congregation that few church leaders have the energy to look much beyond that community. The frenzy of modern life makes it easy for me to forget that the Church is bigger than my small portion of it. I want to feel connected to something larger, but the cost of doing so seems too high. Instead, it is easier to find reasons why I should disregard this or that group. After all, I like my way and my group best. What threatens Church unity, then, is not just conflict, but a deficit of vision and courage. "The Church is One" has become for many, if not most, a utopian ideal, a hope for the next world but not an article of faith for everyday living.

In my third call, I served a small church that was self-sufficient and conservative. The people were loving, mostly faithful in worship, but not inclined to extend themselves much. The younger members, who could have made a difference, were mostly occupied with their full lives outside the church. The aging stalwarts were generally unenthusiastic about trying anything new or engaging anything outside the parish boundaries, yet one of the marks of the Church was very much in evidence in that parish: catholicity. By that I mean what the catechism says: We proclaimed "the whole Faith to all people, to the end of time per Vincent of berins" (the so-called "Vincentian canon" for catholicity). We maintained historical continuity, taught our young people, ministered to all who were in any way affiliated, and observed the entire curriculum that is built into the calendar of the church year, he rhythm of life that goes on generation after generation. We didn't innovate much, but we were faithful and comprehensive.

The problem with that kind of catholicity is that it needs to be balanced by the other marks of the Church: the dynamic of the Holy Spirit, a vision of the Church as one, and especially a sense of the Church's apostolic mission to the world.

"Apostolic" is a word with tethers to the past, but also has present imperatives and future orientation, just like "prophecy." A church is truly apostolic if it remains faithful to the bull's-eye of the Gospel message, obedient to the authority of its Lord in present circumstances, and committed to reaching out to those who are still outside the circle of faith. The apostles were those who were commissioned and sent forth by our risen Lord to spread the Good News of God's love and purposes for all people. They bore witness to what they had experienced, as well as what they had been taught. So we, if we are to be apostolic in our day, must preserve the essential teaching but must also bear witness to what our Lord is doing among us now. If we are only maintaining a historical record and preserving a tradition, like curators of a religious museum, then we are faithless, heedless, and disobedient—as in the parable of the talents (Matt. 25)—the servant who buried his talent instead of investing it was chastised by his master.

The prophets of the old covenant always spoke out of their awareness of what God had previously done and shown, but they addressed their present situation and looked at where things were headed. They considered Israel's place in the world its call to be a "light to the nations," as Isaiah (42:6, 49:6) put it. The separateness in its religious observance that Israel came to insist upon was not an end in itself, but intended as a means of remaining faithful to Israel's identity and purpose as a people who had a covenant with God. So today, a false prophet is one who disregards current abuses and speaks only of a glorious past, or who focuses exclusively on the welfare of some part of the Church and not on the Church's mission of outreach to all people. Truth-telling means facing the whole truth, and not one's preferred part of it.

In my fourth and final congregation, I came into a divided community. Many people had chosen sides between two priests who had recently been dismissed because they could not work together. When I called upon the members, I found I was in many cases doing exit interviews. As I listened to the stories of conflict and what people had liked about each of the priests, I found myself in the curious position of being compared to *two* immediate predecessors, who were about as different from each other as possible: one highly articulate, intellectual, meticulous, organized, and musically gifted; the other amiable, unstructured, liturgically casual, and unhurried—an Anglican parson in the old style, primarily interested in visiting with people. Somehow I had to honor what each had brought to the church, yet move on to address pressing needs in order to fulfill our apostolic commission.

The Church in America today reflects mainstream culture. That is, we are a nation of shoppers, so naturally we are also a nation of church shoppers. Brand names have become less important than price, availability, and service. The culture is awash in a smorgasbord of choices, and shoppers feel quite comfortable making their own eclectic assortment of practices and articles of faith. Although that kind of independence is not entirely a bad thing, it does foster a false view of what church membership means. So long as people see themselves as customers to be satisfied rather than members of a body with an apostolic commission, the orientation of the Church will remain tilted toward "What am I getting?" rather than "What are we called to do?"

In a land of do-it-yourselfers, it is tempting to think that we can compartmentalize the Church and keep it at arm's length, just as we can now do much of our shopping online, without leaving our homes. The apostolic witness of the Church, however, is that "you can't be a Christian by yourself." We need other people to teach us, support us, guide and correct us, just as in home schooling we have not dispensed with the teacher, only reassigned that role to a parent. Though people today may be more fluid in their denominational commitments, it remains true that life in community over time is an essential part of our spiritual formation as members of the Body of Christ. We need the Church and, conversely, the Church needs us in order to be healthy and fully functioning.

A popular illusion is that a group of church people can somehow immunize themselves against cultural infection by avoiding change or breaking contact with other church groups with whom they disagree. The irony is that such avoidance is generally motivated by the desire to perpetuate a standard which has been learned from the culture and that is not—repeat, *not*—an essential part of the apostolic message. The Church should never kid itself into thinking it is unaffected by culture. However, the Church does have the privilege and responsibility of engaging and challenging the culture. To be in the world but not of the world (see John 17:14) means that we are in dialogue with the culture: it is a two-way conversation.

What threatens the Church today is not disagreements with the culture so much as it is a lack of awareness of the real inroads made by culture, for example, the pervasiveness of idolatries such as the American quest for success and the identification of that with impressive buildings, large gatherings of people, and supreme self-confidence. The Church is failing in many places in not being able to distinguish the service of Jesus Christ from the service of ego and security needs. The Church is failing, not always in its visible signs of influence, but in the inability of its members to elevate love and self-giving above confidence and self-satisfaction.

Young people today are torn between the visible signs of success and the authenticity for which they hunger. They seek a true authority, the authority of Jesus, but find that it generally comes packaged with a view of the Church as triumphal, stocked with ready-made answers supposedly based on biblical authority as God's own final pronouncements, rather than a view of the church as servant and pilgrim in a complex and needy world. So if you are a young person today, where do you go: to your parents' church, which is clearly struggling to maintain itself, or to your friends' church, which is upbeat, confident, contemporary, and authoritative in its denunciation of what it sees as cultural perversions, such as modification of traditional views of marriage and family? What do you do if you are a young person discovering that what comes naturally to you is defined as a perversion in your friends' church, while it is never discussed in your parents' church?

It's time to face how messed up we are as a culture immersed in issues of sexuality, with the Church itself as very much part of the problem. That's what being apostolic calls us to do.

Yours with the courage to look at what is really going on,

Letter 5

Humans As Sexual Beings:
A Fresh Look at a Sensitive Topic

Dear Sexual Being:

Does that form of address seem overly familiar? Thank you for your patience with me, as I have been laying the foundation upon which we may construct a Christian dwelling open to all, but are you upset with me that I am now calling attention to your sexuality? I'm sorry, but this topic is one elephant in the living room around which we must not tiptoe.

Dear sexual being . . . "Are you talking to *me?*" . . . Yes, I am talking to *you*. Are you afraid of owning that part of yourself? Listen to these foundational words: "God created humankind in his image, in the image of God he created them; male and female he created them" (Gen. 1:27). "God saw everything that he had made, and indeed, it was very good" (Gen. 1:31).

Sexuality is a part of who we are; it is not just a matter of what we do. Some pious Christians would prefer to compartmentalize sex, just as some would prefer to compartmentalize religion—that is, make it one part of their lives separate from the rest of their lives. However, that is not how religious faith works, and that is not how sexuality works. We bring our sexual identity and feelings with us every place we go—not blatantly, perhaps, but as an influential part of ourselves, always present whether we recognize it or not.

One view of sex is that it is a necessary evil, and that God doesn't want us to think about it except at very specific and necessary times. Let me ask you this: Who do you think invented sex? More

doi:10.1300/5661_05

important, why was sex invented? Was it only for the perpetuation of the species, or might sex have other purposes as well? Might it not be another part of the rich banquet of creation that we are to celebrate and manage wisely, as Genesis 1 sets forth our role in regard to the rest of creation? Everything that God has created is good, including our sexuality. The author of Genesis 1 took pains to emphasize that by repeating it several times.

It is quite true that sex may become a false god, just as money and other forms of power may easily usurp God's throne. It is also quite true that sex can become an addiction, as television and gambling and alcohol and food and dieting and anger and shopping and work can become addictions. Part of what makes sex so tempting, though, is the way we have made it highly visible yet unmentionable.

Many people take the view that if we don't talk about something we can keep people, especially young people, from thinking about it, but if that doesn't work with the other elephants—such as prejudice, death, and the obscene and growing gap between wealth and poverty—why should it work with this elephant? Sure, if we talk too much about sex we might lead people to think it is more important than it really is, but if we *don't* talk about it, what will people think *then?* Just to talk about sex at all is, in the minds of some, to give it a legitimacy it doesn't deserve, as a second-class part of God's creation, ranking somewhere around the process of eliminating waste products from our bodies. Their attitude becomes "Let's not talk about it; people might get the wrong idea." What would that wrong idea be?

Some hold the view that the Church is or should be asexual, as though that is more "holy" than being sexual. However, what "holy" really means is not "removed from the physical world" but "dedicated to God." Everything in our lives should be so dedicated.

Here is where we are, as a culture in nominally Christian America today: conflicted, hypocritical, fearful, and confused. On the one hand, we package sex as a commodity and use it to sell all sorts of other commodities, including politicians, cars, health products, clothes, physical fitness and diet, and leisure pursuits. On the other hand, we treat sex as a shameful secret to be hidden from our children, even when they already know about it. We have intense curiosity about what other people are doing sexually; we can't admit it, however, even to ourselves in many cases. Look at the tabloid coverage given to the sexual misbehavior of public figures. The copious detail and outcries are extreme, because so is the popular interest. Thus, while we are a remarkably open culture in terms of the many freedoms we allow, there is a puritanical impulse in contemporary America that would seek to shield all of us, not just the children, from admitting any sexual thoughts or feelings outside the bedrooms of state-sanctioned or church-sanctioned marriage.

We could contrast America with Europe, which blends a militantly secular culture with vestiges of Christian faith and arrives at a more tolerant acceptance of sexuality as a fact of life, neither overrating nor underrating it. We might also look at Islamic cultures, where sexuality is sustained at a high level of erotic energy, but is kept strictly private. America, which exhibits a wide range of sexual attitudes, seems to be schizophrenic. There is much public exhibitionism and preoccupation with sex, but also much public outcry whenever anyone goes "too far."

How did we become a culture so sexually liberated on the one hand, while being so sexually repressed on the other? In the United States we are not two different cultures where sex is concerned, but a single, pervasively confused culture. How did we become so conflicted about such a fundamental part of life? The short answer is *fear*, compounded by envy and religious hegemony in spite of our professed religious tolerance. Because sex *is* an important part of life and we all have an interest in it, both societal and personal, we are afraid at multiple levels.

Yes, sex is dangerous, as religion is dangerous, because of the powerful feelings it arouses and the actions that may follow. Sex is dangerous, but so is the automobile—and we hand the car keys to sixteen-year-olds. Sex is dangerous—so what do we do? We encourage abstinence, conveniently forgetting (or perhaps remembering too well) the feelings triggered by our own hormones when we were teenagers, and we fail to provide backup support in the form of protection against disease and pregnancy.

What do we think we are teaching our young people—that sex is holy and should be reserved for marriage? Or are we teaching them that sex is so powerful and scary that we can't even talk about it, and we would prefer that they wouldn't, either. Obviously, we don't handle alcohol extremely well as a society, and sex can be at least as intoxicating as alcohol— even more so, when sex is inflamed by the use of alcohol or drugs. It's difficult to keep alcohol out of the hands of teenagers, and it's just as difficult to keep them from satisfying their curiosity about sex—especially when it is so patently obvious that we are a sex-obsessed society, both in the media coverage and in the prohibitions.

The societal management (or mismanagement) of sex has been going on in Jewish and Christian cultures for a long time. At first, the concern reflected in the Hebrew scriptures was that God's people be as fertile as possible, so as to multiply and occupy the land. Human fertility was like agriculture: every seed had to be deployed for maximum yield. Onan was not chastised for masturbation, as too many Bible readers believe, but for refusing to fulfill his duty of fathering children for his deceased brother (Gen. 38:9). Multiple wives were perfectly fine, as long as they were obtained in legitimate ways. Women and children were a form of property and having a number of them was a sign of divine blessing.

If procreation for the extension of a society was the prime purpose of sex, then anything that stood in the way of such fertility was to be frowned upon. This view of sexuality carried over into the church and has persisted long after we have seen that expanding the population is no longer the greatest good for human society.

A related issue is individual choice in sex and family planning versus societal interest in the management of sex for the common good. We have laws to protect individuals, but also to protect what we see as the best interests of society, keeping sexual exposure within some limits and sexual acts of a predatory nature strictly off limits. We are, of course, not all in agreement as to what behaviors should be ruled out of bounds, especially when it comes to reproductive matters.

Desire for control over the sexual activity of others is, unfortunately, not motivated solely by concern for the common good. It is all too often an imposition of personal religious beliefs upon others who do not share those beliefs, and regrettably, it is often energized by the concern that someone else may be having too much fun, or at least more fun than I am having. Puritan dress may be out of style, but puritanical attitudes are still very much in fashion. For example, a man and a woman who are friends outside of marriage will find themselves regarded with close scrutiny if they enjoy being together too much or too often. Such concern may have a realistic element, but likely also contains some measure of projection, as onlookers ascribe their own temptations to another. Although envy is still listed as one of the seven deadly sins, it often comes dressed in the guise of protecting decent society.

Was St. Paul antisex? Did he dislike or distrust women? With regard to the latter question, passages from his epistles may be cited on both sides. Paul certainly valued and included women among his friends and ministry colleagues, as evidenced by his personal greetings at the conclusion of Romans, I Corinthians, and Colossians, and his sending best wishes to "brothers and sisters" in nearly every letter. Yet Paul urged women to cover their heads in church (1 Cor. 11), and Paul, or more likely one of his followers, barred women from the ministry of teaching or headship over men (1 Tim. 2:12). In Galatians 3:28, however, we hear Paul's ringing call to equality in the Gospel: "There is no longer Jew or Greek, there is no longer slave or free, there is no longer male or female; for all of you are one in Christ Jesus."

Paul himself did not marry, and he urged those able to exercise such self-discipline to refrain from marrying, in light of the urgency and priority of the Gospel message over personal concerns and the expectation of the imminent Second Coming of Christ. Yet he thought it better for Christians to marry than to be "aflame with passion" (1 Cor. 7:9). He wrote, "It is well for a man not to touch a woman" (1 Cor. 7:1). However, in marriage he thought it important for husband and wife to have their "conjugal rights" (1 Cor. 7:3). Evidently for Paul, sex was a distraction from the work of the Church. Subsequent generations of devoted Church leaders, following that line of thought, extolled celibacy as a "higher calling" than marriage. The Church's subsequent endorsement of clerical celibacy, however, had an economic element as well: priests who could have no offspring could not convey church property to their heirs.

Although Paul's views of sex and marriage were ambivalent, it was his successors—living when Christ's Second Coming was no longer seen as imminent—who institutionalized the view that sex and marriage were for those otherwise unable to control themselves.

What about Jesus? Do we have any clues as to his view of sexuality and women? He talked about marriage and divorce and adultery, but aside from one mention of lust in Matthew (5:28), one each of licentiousness and fornication in Mark (7:21-22), and a mention of the prodigal son's dissolute living with prostitutes in Luke (15:30), the Gospels do not depict a savior preoccupied with the dangers of sex; instead, the threat he speaks of most often is the lure of possessions.

As for his relationships with women, Jesus appears to have been accepting, even egalitarian: witness his friendship with Mary and Martha of Bethany, his close relationship to Mary Magdalene—how close is a matter of speculation—and his extended conversation with the woman of Samaria in John 4, which is the longest conversation Jesus has with anyone in the Gospels.

Sex is more of a problem for Bible readers today than it was for the people in the Bible, or those who wrote the Bible. Sex is one more of life's many good but problematical gifts: problematical because it requires some judgment in the use of human freedom, yet good because of its creative energy and potential for blessing. That is no less true for gay couples than for heterosexual couples.

What are some things sex is good for, besides procreation? Sex is part of the lab work for our social, emotional, and spiritual development. It is not just about maintaining the species, but about reaching out in relationship. Sex and spirit are not opposites: they are part of one yearning toward wholeness. The real opposites in life are not body and spirit, but drawing apart versus coming together—what kills community versus what nurtures community.

Sex isn't just about the individual with sexual urges. It involves considerations of the partner, the circumstance, the terms of endearment. We should not minimize the sexual yearning by labeling it as simply glandular; neither should we minimize the factor of another human consciousness in the "love object," a human being whose feelings may be quite different from our own.

A body is a gift, as time is a gift and consciousness is a gift. No two sexual beings are exactly alike, because sexuality involves mind and body, spirit and impulse. That element of freedom is not to be equated with narcissism, which has wells of life apart from sexuality. Narcissism can be asexual, or it can use sexuality as a means of self-aggrandizement. The point is, sexuality by its very nature points to *relationship* and is not exclusively centered on the self. In fact, sex has enormous sacramental capacity—that is, the capacity to be an outward and visible sign of inner feelings and intentions. For a married couple, sexual intimacy can say, "I love you, I need you, you are a part of me." As we reach out for union with another human being, we acknowledge not only our neediness but perhaps also something of our quest for union with God. As the lover in the Song of Solomon (3:1) says: "Upon my bed at night I sought him whom my soul loves; I sought him, but found him not; I called him, but he gave no answer."

Sex is a kind of power, but it is not all about power. It is also about appreciation. It is about communion, sharing of feeling, being less alone in the universe. Sex becomes problematical, even for mature adults, because as communion it requires some measure of agreement between human beings in terms of its timing and manner of expression. Feelings cannot be easily turned on or off at will. Nor are such feelings independent of the ego and one's self-esteem. To be rejected at any time is painful and may deter or postpone further attempts at reaching out. The word "intimacy" is used advisedly with regard to sexual expression. More than skin is exposed when one is aroused, and more than flesh is required for complete satisfaction.

Sex, in other words, is bound up with important developmental and maintenance needs such as caring, self-expression, self-esteem, and human connection at multiple levels. In terms of Abraham Maslow's hierarchy of human needs, sex encompasses the spiritual as well as the physical, and it ranges from simple relief of tension to higher levels such as love, esteem, aesthetic appreciation, and self-actualization. It is no wonder that interpreters of the Song of Solomon have taken the celebration of human love and longing there expressed as an extended metaphor characterizing the relationship between God and the covenant people. Sex makes use of all our human capacities: tenderness, strength, imagination, the use of our senses, and our use of symbols. It calls forth not just our lowest impulses but also our highest impulses, such as generosity and the desire to lose ourselves in another.

In any truly committed relationship, sex is interactive with all kinds of things going on in the life of the couple: work stresses, ego injuries, questions about the meaning of life, and outside relationships that are anxiety-producing or life-draining. When a couple can incorporate sex as a resource for facing those stresses, sex can be restorative, bringing hope, peace, communion, and enhanced self-esteem. If communication in the marriage is inadequate, sex may present itself as one more demand, rather than a form of ministry or therapy or supplemental communication. Most couples, at any given time, are moving either in a positive direction of intimacy and affirmation, incorporating their sexual expression, or in a negative direction, where avoidance of intimacy reinforces feelings of isolation and distress.

In marriage and in life, our sexuality is not just about what we do but about who we are and how we feel about ourselves. It is certainly not all of who we are. Thus sexuality should be neither denied nor exalted, but integrated, celebrated, and dedicated to the service of God, as we consecrate the many other gifts that have been entrusted to us.

Gifts of God often come disguised as challenges, waiting to be embraced before they can produce valuable learnings. One of the most popular shows on television from 2003 to 2005 was *Joan of Arcadia,* about a teenage girl and her family. Although every member of the family is challenged by events in the school and community, only Joan has the peculiar privilege of being visited by God each episode and given her own special assignment. These assignments are never easy and generally do not go smoothly. Joan is not pleased when God shows up in some new human disguise and says, "Joan, I want you to. . . ."

The assignment usually makes no sense to Joan up front, yet time and again, as she reluctantly obeys, Joan finds that her assignment puts her in a position to befriend someone. In the process, Joan also gains something—not a tidy little moral, but a greater appreciation of what it means to be a caring human being among so many human souls who are as overwhelmed as she generally feels.

What Joan discovers is that God knows things about the human condition that we human beings haven't learned yet. Our first impressions of what is going on fall way short of a comprehensive view of what God is doing, even in our own lives. So we learn along with Joan about the limits of human judgment.

God's view of life is larger than ours, even when we think we have the benefits of the best scriptural guidance. Our discomfort with some element of life, such as some human sexual tendency, does not imply that God is similarly displeased. It is so tempting to say that what is uncomfortable for me is therefore unnatural, and so cannot be part of God's plan, but among the truths we are learning about human sexuality is the great variation among human beings, even those who are exclusively heterosexual in their practices. Like Joan, we should be gaining some reticence about prejudging situations from the outside.

At times it seems that sex is one of God's jokes on the human race. Certainly it produces a lot of pain and confusion as it is presented to us through the conflicted norms of American culture and the voices of the media. Young males endowed with raging testosterone are told for many years: "Look, but don't you dare touch!" Young females are often told: "You must make yourself desirable, but don't you dare let anyone satisfy that desire with you!" Gay and lesbian youth and adults may be told: "Your desire is even more ridiculous and offensive than normal desires, so you *really* can't act on it!" Lost in this wilderness of fear and folly is any remembrance of the essential goodness of God's creation, or the dignity of human beings as moral agents made in the image of God.

Sexuality and spirituality may be related in more than one way. They may be placed in opposition to one another, in a reversion to Greek dualism, which is *not* biblical. In this view, the Church tends to be seen as the enforcer of socially approved sexual behavior, and homosexual relationships are ruled out as incompatible with traditional Christian teaching. Another way, which *is* biblical, is to see sexuality as an expression of relationship, including divine-human relationship. In this view, sexuality and spirituality are partners, and both are a divine gift. Either can be misused, and so corrupt the other, or they can be mutually reinforcing, as in the case of same-sex partners who demonstrate in their long-term committed relationship a fidelity that mirrors the faithfulness of God.

It's time now to hear from some of those beautiful people who are like you and me in yearning to love and be loved, but who are drawn to partners of the same gender. Are you ready to hear their stories?

Yours in the mystery of life and love
and the creation of seen and unseen,

Letter 6

What Are Gay People Like?

Dear Confused Church Member:

Do you know any gay people? If you're not sure, the answer is "yes." They are professionals in your community, friends you knew in high school and college, people who advise you, people who go to your church. Very possibly you have a relative who is gay. Maybe some of these people are still "in the closet," or maybe they just haven't "come out" to you, because they weren't sure how you would react.

The fact that you haven't yet noticed the sexual orientation of these folks says as much about them as it does about you: namely, they aren't that much different from anyone else. In fact, there is as great a range of variation among homosexuals as there is among heterosexuals. You might want to read Bruce Bawer's book, *A Place at the Table* (1993), on that score. People are so much *more* than their sex lives.

If you would like to get a clearer picture of what gay people are like—what they are thinking, what their experience has been—the best way is to *ask* them, after they have gotten to know you. That's what I did. With their permission, I'm going to share some things gay people I know told me about how they discovered they were "different" in their sexual feelings and how others reacted when that became known. Before I get started, though, I need to make a couple of points.

The first is a matter of language. Let's get rid of the word "lifestyle" as a way of classifying people, specifically GLBT people. "Lifestyle" implies a *chosen* way of being in the world. As I hope

doi:10.1300/5661_06

55

will become clear, people *don't* choose to be gay, or bisexual, or even transgendered. Instead, they *discover* at some point that they are oriented sexually and affectionately in a way that goes against the cultural grain. So let's call their leaning an "orientation." The word "lifestyle" is inaccurate and prejudicial; it presupposes facts not in evidence. When I hear the word "lifestyle" in connection with GLBT people, I know I am listening to someone who, at the least, is uninformed.

The second point is based on a general truth I learned from a psychiatrist in one of my former congregations. He taught me that any human behavior or characteristic can be placed on a continuum, that is, a range, with two extremes and a midpoint. It's helpful to think of sexual orientation this way; it avoids many errors we might otherwise make.

Toward one end of the continuum are people who are so firmly heterosexual that they could never be attracted to a person of the same gender. Toward the other end of the continuum are people who cannot be attracted to anyone *except* persons of the same gender. Around the midrange are persons we call "bisexual," who can form sexual and affectional bonds (i.e., fall in love) with *either* males or females. Now here is the interesting part: between the midrange and the ends of the continuum are some persons who *might* be attracted to someone against their normal orientation, under the right circumstances. That possibility scares some young adults who may recall "experimenting" when younger.

When I hear claims that some organization, usually church-related, has "converted" someone from homosexual to heterosexual orientation, I know that one of two things has happened. One is that the person so converted was somewhere around the midrange, so was able to "switch" attraction without any great strain. The other likelihood is that all that has changed is behavior—for an indefinite period—not the fundamental orientation. We already know that sexual feelings can be sublimated, and sexual energy rechanneled, for example, into serving God. We also know that many celibate clergy have failed in that attempt over the long run. We also know—although the "ex-gay" organizations who boast of converting people will never admit this—that many who have claimed conversion later "fell off the wagon" and reverted to practicing their true sexual orientation, which *never changed*. Incidentally, we don't need to worry that heterosexuals will be converted to homosexuality, either.

Not so long ago I had the discomfiting experience of listening to a man in midlife—a husband, father, and member of an evangelical church—tell how supportive his wife was of his continuing struggle against his homosexual urges, which had first surfaced in junior high. He offered himself as a role model and counselor for young men fighting against this "sin." I wanted to cry, seeing what his church had done to him.

In this time when GLBT people are the last group in society that many church people believe they can stigmatize without guilt, the real heroes are those courageous, honest, faithful, and generous people who have come to accept that God made them "different" and have gone on to hold their heads up as responsible citizens, many of them as active church members. They are some of the finest Christians I have known.

Here is part of the story of Elena, who grew up in a small Midwest town as a member of a conservative church. Church was important to her, but as she grew older she became uncomfortable with the way women were treated in her church. The answers to her questions about how the Bible was being used were not very satisfactory. She became ambivalent about Christianity.

Her first experience that hinted at her sexual orientation was, as it turned out, also a spiritual experience. She remembers the day vividly. She was sitting on her porch swing at 7:00 p.m. on a hot summer day. Suddenly clouds began to roll in, the light changed, the church roof nearby began to glow, and it started to rain in big drops. She ran out into the street to dance with Lana, her best friend. Then she jumped on her bike to go watch the sunset. A wind came up. She felt she had abandoned reason and embraced nature. She got soaking wet and raced home, full of joy. She threw her clothes in the washer, wrapped herself in a sheet, and lay out in the rain in the backyard. Lana came streaking out and lay naked under the sheet with her. They didn't touch each other, just enjoyed companionship as they shared an experience of the world.

Lana's parents decided to take her away from Elena after that summer and send her to another school. Before they did, however, the girls went to the big city and got tattoos. Elena had wanted the new moon with three stars, but graciously yielded it to Lana and got the butterfly instead. She says that Lana is "marked forever" by that summer and the gift of the tattoo.

After Lana was taken away, Elena was grieving, and a gay male friend said to her: "Of *course* you're upset; she broke your heart." Elena realized that it takes a great force to break one's heart. She knew then that she had loved Lana, and she wanted a force in her life—love—that was powerful enough to break a heart.

She came out as a lesbian in college at age nineteen, realizing that she had always resonated with women, experientially and spiritually, and that she was attracted especially to older women. Her first sexual contacts with men, previous to college, had been unsatisfactory. When she exchanged her first lesbian kiss, several months later, she recalls: "If we had not been lying down, I would have fallen over." This was a confirmation of what she had been feeling. It was the missing piece in her passionate nature. It seemed that God had played a trick on her—not the trick of denying her a sexual passion, but of giving her a passion that she had to *find*. Of course, she soon came to learn that "the first woman you kiss *doesn't* love you, *doesn't* want to spend the rest of her life with you."

As Elena further explored her sexuality, she found that she couldn't relax in a sexual relationship unless the person she was with *did* love her. She could give pleasure but not really have satisfaction in a casual encounter. She came to understand, "I had started on this adventure because of love." For a while she took a vow of celibacy and made herself "hard to get."

When she finally met her partner for life, it was another spiritual experience. Elena made the first move, following the woman and calling out, "Hey, you! I can't call you by name, because I don't *know* your name!" The woman's name was Karen, and it turned out that Karen was a believing Christian. That first evening they danced. The next day they got together, and as Elena was primping in a mirror, Karen suddenly became aware that she had previously seen Elena's face in a vision, at an event that was their *wedding*.

Elena decided to break her vow of celibacy. She was able to give herself to Karen because she trusted her. Within two weeks, Karen proposed. A mystical element was present in their relationship from the outset. Elena had a dream in which she was walking up a path. When she turned around, she saw herself following herself, but dressed differently and carrying a silver urn. "It was the old me, the me from the past," and the silver urn represented all her grief of love lost.

"One thing I love about the church," Elena says, "is the way that faith is a time machine. Love is a time machine, too—the past, present, and future are all together." She says that fear of loss can keep one from giving herself in love. "But unless you accept the loss, you can't get the love. I have learned more about God, Jesus, love, spirituality, everything, from being with someone who loves me. Sexuality is minuscule, in the shadow cast by overwhelming love." (If you are thinking that Elena may one day be a preacher, I suspect you are right.) In light of this new vision, the nature worship to which Elena had been attracted in her transition years no longer had much pull.

Elena was not able to discuss her sexual orientation with her family, except with her younger brother years later. She has some things, though, to say to the Church, so we will return to her in the next letter, but now I want to share a story that has not yet yielded much in the way of a blessing.

Michael was raised Roman Catholic. He attended church with his family and was interested in spirituality until he began to experience conflict in junior high. He had realized as a child that he was gay, and he came out in junior high. Then a sexuality unit was taught in church school, and homosexuality was labeled as wrong. Michael cried himself to sleep, night after night. Many of his friends were supportive, though.

By his freshman year of college, he began exploring other types of spirituality, even while he was working as a church organist. He came out to his family during spring break, and their reaction was "overwhelmingly negative." They said he was "confused," in need of counseling. They gave him materials that indicated he could change. He decided it was worth a try. Fundamentalist friends worked on him, and he entered an ex-gay program in another community. He was drawn there not only by the curriculum but by the promise of having a church family already in place. He was encouraged to explore the *causes* of his "homosexuality." Being gay was seen by his counselors as a defilement, something in his past, not to be spoken of. He then attended a two-year Bible school on the West Coast. He got involved with a girl, but was not really attracted to her, except as a friend.

Throughout Michael's ten-year involvement with the ex-gay ministry he maintained a secret life—no relationships, just pornography. Eventually he had to face the fact that his feelings hadn't changed. He also longed for someone to love, someone with whom he could spend his life.

Relocating to a Midwest college town, Michael got involved with a gay men's discussion group on campus. Previous to that he had felt neither a part of the gay community nor the Christian community. After a ten-year detour in his life—essentially the decade of his twenties—Michael now finds himself back where he was as a college freshman, starting all over again.

The Church people who worked with Michael all that time were insistent and aggressive; they didn't want to accept "failure." The only options given to Michael were celibacy or pretending. Michael now says plaintively, "I didn't choose this, and I made a good faith effort for ten years to change." What he was finally told by Evangelical Christians was: "This may be your lot in life—to suffer." He read online this statement by a gay Mormon, which summed up the Evangelical approach: "Optimistic denial of the truth takes precedence over reality." That has certainly been Michael's experience.

Another gay man who found the church to be no real help to him in dealing with his sexual orientation is Edward, who grew up back East as a black Southern Baptist. He began to struggle with sexuality issues around age twelve. His church had a youth fellowship, and one day they were talking about sex and putting anonymous questions into a question box. When the pastor drew out the question Edward had put in, he told the group: "Homosexuals are our friends . . . but they are *sick*." This was the voice of authority, and all the authorities—school, church, and home, even the teen help line—agreed: "This behavior is not acceptable."

So Edward became the class clown. He says, "I became one of the lost folks." When he heard a warning about going into the men's restroom at the public library, he went there immediately. He began "cruising" at age fourteen. Edward says, "I grew up with a God of damnation, and to this day I'm afraid of lightning"—because lightning means "God is doing his work."

Edward knew he had to leave home, so he went to college in the Midwest, a long way from home. In those days, cruising *was* the gay life, Edward says. Straight people could comprehend gay cruising better than they could comprehend gay committed relationships. Finally, because of his growing fear of AIDS, Edward renounced gay sex. He also was finally able to come out. He began to study and to reexamine the biblical grounds against homosexuality. A philosopher told him, though: "Ideas don't change people; relationships do."

As he looks back on his lonely journey now, Edward observes: "A lot of gay energy and talent is being diverted" to deal with the issues occasioned by societal attitudes. He says, "I'm blessed with the perspective of being gay. . . . I can't take so many things for granted. The struggle has brought me riches. It has inflamed my spirit and set my intellect on fire."

Rory, now retired, has had an easier road than Edward. He sees himself as "one of the lucky ones," considering the time in which he grew up. He was blessed in his parents and friends, accepted as a person, not excluded. That continued in the armed forces. Of course, Rory did not go out of his way to identify himself as gay. In fact, he never really thought about the implications of his emotional life until some years later, when he found that his feelings toward a male friend were not reciprocated. A gay friend then helped him to come out. As a member of a large urban parish in the East, Rory felt comfortable as an identified gay man. Some years later, though, he moved to the Midwest, where he was surprised to see how closeted the gay Christians were. It was ten years before he felt free to come out in his new setting, and then only with selected people.

Sharon grew up knowing she was different, but with no means to interpret her feelings. Finally, in college, a roommate confronted her with the reality of her sexual orientation. However, when she shared this discovery with her best friend, the friend—who later turned out to be lesbian also—walked out on her.

She couldn't talk to the clergy, at first. Finally she talked to a pastor and found him supportive, but the intolerance of Church teaching was so ingrained in her that she couldn't shake it. When she told another good friend about her orientation, she was told she was going to hell. From that Sharon learned: don't tell anyone. She says, "I knew I would have to live in a minority of silence, and I could not live with it." She turned to heavy drinking and drug use. Church seemed hopeless, so she dropped out.

Sharon relocated to another city to take a job and thought she would try to be straight. She had dates, but it was never very comfortable. One guy she dated turned out to be a drug dealer. She moved in with a divorced man who did drugs, despite the fact that he was a recovering alcoholic. She started dating a woman, also, who turned out to be violent.

When Sharon moved to a larger city to get away, she was "pretty well messed up." She was still in an abusive relationship with the woman. She talked to God, as she had when she was a lonely child, and asked God to remove her loneliness and to show himself, so she could have God as a friend. She was rescued from her alcoholism by community agencies and by a friend who encouraged her and steered her toward Alcoholics Anonymous.

In order to stay sober, Sharon had to leave her old drinking subculture, which included her gay friends. She says, "I was tired of the secrets." She decided to go home and come out to her parents, who had wondered about but had never discussed her orientation, even with each other. She has worked since "to be the good daughter." She has also found a life partner and an accepting church, and is now happy and sober.

Like Sharon, Doug turned to drinking and drugging out of his sense of not belonging anywhere as a young gay man. He was nearly thirty before he was able to talk to his sisters about his sexual orientation—the first family members in whom he confided. It turned out they already knew. He didn't come out to his parents until he was thirty-eight and in a personal crisis, and they got the news this way: "Guess what? I'm a thief, I'm drunk, and I'm gay." His mother did not handle it well. His father came to terms with it within twenty-four hours. To this day his mother remains conflicted; though she tries to be loving, she still believes that gays can change.

Into his early twenties Doug taught Sunday school and sang in the choir, until alcohol took over. He was nearly forty and sober for a year before he got back to the church, after a "God experience" his third time in treatment. When he turned his life over to God, he felt a physical energy come through him and a peace come over him. From that time on, no matter what would happen, he felt "I'm . . . in a protective bubble."

Prior to that time Doug had seen God as very judgmental. Then he found a church that openly welcomed gays and was racially diverse. Doug felt immediately known and accepted, and began to hear a gospel of unconditional love. He became more open about his sexual orientation outside the Church, as well. When Matthew Shepard was beaten to death, Doug decided that he needed to come out at work. He says, "They needed to know that they knew a gay person." Though Doug told his boss, prior to coming out, that he was a little fearful for his safety, he found a surprising protector in a co-worker named Matt, who was "a very scary-looking guy, about 6'4" and 300 pounds, with a mullet haircut, tattoos, a leather vest, an earring, a deep gravelly voice, and gruff demeanor." Matt was straight, but had a lesbian friend. Because of Matt's support, Doug got no negative feedback from anyone after he came out. Matt had basically put out the word, "Don't f—— with this guy." One Christian at work did begin to evangelize Doug, but in a gentle and respectful way, actually listening and trying to understand.

Not all subsequent co-workers would respond that way. When he moved to another city, a female co-worker in his new job felt compelled to warn him that he would go to hell if he didn't repent.

Doug has tried to love her, even so. He says that he has been less affected by encounters with homophobic individuals than by "the whole heterosexist system." Just as with white racism, the system is invisible to the privileged.

I'll share one more story before we move on. This one could easily be a letter all by itself. I'll let Kevin introduce his own story.

I've been gay my entire life. I can remember things back to a very young age. I grew up the youngest in a large family, and I tend to remember many things that my older siblings have long forgotten. I can honestly remember having gay feelings when I was as young as four years old.

When I was five, our family purchased our first TV. We received one station fine most of the time, but on Monday nights we'd turn to Channel 5 and watch *All-Star Wrestling* on a snowy screen. It was my favorite show of the week. When you throw in Tarzan and anything to do with gladiators, you get the picture. I've always found the male body to be, shall we say, "warming." On the other side of the fence, *Playboy* never did a thing for me.

When I was ten, my family moved to a small town. Throughout my teen years, I "experimented" in many ways with many other boys my age. . . . I thought all boys "experimented" and something clicked in their heads when they became men and they became heterosexual. In my case—no click. What is interesting, most of these boys turned into husbands and fathers, with the exception of one or two. What's even more interesting is the number of males my age that I *didn't* experiment with who later turned out to be gay. . . ."

During my two years in business college, sex was on the back burner. Close to the time of my graduation, a boy I grew up with called and asked me over to his home. He had heard that I liked to experiment, and one thing led to another—very quickly. I remember for about a week afterward I didn't want anything to do with sex—then he called again.

Throughout the following two years I came out to the gay community. I met a lot of gay people. . . . During this time I was asked out on lots of dates, by men and by women. The women I dated were interested in marriage and sex. I was interested in the marriage portion, but sex with women was something I definitely didn't enjoy and found repulsive. I stepped up to the plate on a number of occasions, waiting for the click—no click. . . . I can remember being sick to my stomach afterward on most of those encounters. Dating a man, on the other hand, was exciting, fun, warm, and something to look forward to and remember the next day. To me, it was the natural way of doing things. Too, it was the only honest way of doing things. I eventually dropped dating women completely and spent my time with women at work and men at night.

Kevin met his life partner-to-be at age twenty-three, and they developed a close relationship from the very first meeting. Frank was older, married, and had children. Kevin says, "Though we knew it was special, we dealt with the realism of the situation." Kevin dated him regularly and saw other men from time to time.

Meanwhile, Kevin developed a close friendship with a woman at work. She was in a bad marriage. One day as they were driving back from a business conference in another city, she confided that her husband was getting jealous of their friendship. As Kevin puts it,

> I was giving her all the things a woman wants in a man, someone to talk to, laugh with, share common interests, lunch with, and he was giving her the indifference and sex. . . . I told her to tell him I was gay and laughed. She responded, "Are you?" We drove for quite a few miles in total silence. Finally she said again, "Are you?" and I responded, "Does it make a difference?" She said, "No." I told her I was—was she happy now? She said yes. We drove in silence the rest of the way.
>
> The next day all the people in the computer department where I worked, men and women, made it a point to come up to me—to hug or touch me, smile and wink—they all knew, and it felt great. These people were my true friends, and it didn't go beyond them—as far as I knew.

Ten years later, during a short recess in his relationship with Frank—"I was tired of being a third wheel and wanted more in a relationship; I wanted a full-time partner"—Kevin came to a crisis in his life. Arrested in a police sting operation, along with twenty-six other gay men who had been surreptitiously meeting in a restroom at a public park, Kevin received counsel from understanding clergy, resisted a strong temptation to suicide, and decided "the bastards are not going to get me." A guided meditation gave him an experience of divine acceptance. After that, he came out to all his friends and most of his siblings. His mother got some good counsel and found her way to acceptance. His father never spoke of it, but Kevin learned from his siblings after his father's death how much his dad had respected his courage.

Kevin's employer—a family corporation—decided not to fire him, despite the publicity. He received support from other unlikely sources, including some construction workers working nearby, with whom he shared his story. Like his father, they were impressed with his courage. Some of them became close friends and stayed in touch for many years.

When he met with his lawyer, who asked him what he was doing at the park, Kevin said,

> I told him I was looking for another gay person to have sex with—it was the place for gay people to meet other gay people. He got up from his desk, offered me his hand and told me I was the first honest person he'd ever met.

The psychiatrist whom Kevin was required by the court to see as a condition of pretrial diversion announced that Kevin was "the sanest person he'd ever met." Kevin concludes that part of his story:

> I was now completely out of the closet, and a short time later Frank left his wife and moved in with me. We have been an openly gay couple since. I was once told that coming out of the closet was like being drafted into the military. You hate it while it is happening, but are glad and proud about it after it is over.

Kevin's church experience over the years has been mixed. He began attending a small Congregational church at the age of ten with no encouragement from his parents, who were not churchgoers. He felt that he learned some important concepts there. Homosexuality was never discussed. After Kevin met Frank, he joined him at a liturgical church. In general, the people of local congregations have been very supportive. Kevin has some issues with the larger Church, however, and to those we will return.

I think it can be generalized from the foregoing stories and others I have heard, that the label of "homosexual" has been a source of shame for young people who have found themselves to be gay, and that the Church has been the prime teacher and enforcer of that sense of shame, either by silence or by specific teaching. Shame, as John Bradshaw and others have pointed out, is more than guilt: it is not a failure in behavior, but a stain upon one's being—a sense of being a defective model in God's creation that the Church at least doesn't seem to know what to do with, except to try to change or to hide. We will explore more of what the Church has been doing, and what it might do, in the next epistle.

Yours in the ministry of listening and understanding,

Letter 7

What Do Gay People Want?

Dear Concerned Church Member:

You have read some stories now about the experiences of gay and lesbian people. What do they want, especially from the Church? Although there is always a risk in generalizing, the best way to find out is to ask some of them. What is it like to live in a culture and a church that is profoundly heterosexist and generally unaware of that?

Kevin tells us,

> Nothing, and I mean nothing, maddens me more than hearing the word "agenda." Yes, we have an agenda—we want to be treated like human beings. We've always been good enough to play the organ, or sing in the choir, or clean the church, or fix lunch for one hundred, or be your most active members, or give to the plate, but not good enough to be treated like simple human beings. It is almost like the good Christians of the church don't realize we have feelings, too. It must come as a surprise to them that we get hurt. And no, we don't deserve it.

Here is a short summary of the many answers I have heard. Gay and lesbian people want equal treatment, an end to the double standard between straight and gay people. They want to be seen as more than sexual beings. They are multifaceted and complicated like the rest of us. They want an end to persecution and discrimination, especially that which is administered in God's name and that which affects their livelihood, their health, and their freedom.

doi:10.1300/5661_07

The gay people I have known receive signals over and over that they are at the bottom of the pecking order—not as individuals, because many of them are quite accomplished and respected, so "exceptions" are made for them—but as a class within the social order. Because of that awareness, some have chosen to live permanently in the closet. Others have found that it is *death* to hide who they really are, making the pain and risk of coming out a price worth paying. Often this coming out has been delayed many years in order to raise a family conceived while the lesbian or gay person was either in the closet or not yet fully aware of his or her orientation.

Harold grew up isolated in nearly every respect, the youngest child, with no siblings close in age. He was told he was a "mistake." He was a farm kid and attended a conservative ethnic church. From an early age he knew that he was different, but didn't know how. His parents didn't talk much, and he never heard the word "love" in his household. At church he was always the one chosen to sing or recite memory verses. Kids called him "Holy Harold."

Sex information was unavailable to him, until one day his Sunday school teacher, a former Navy chaplain, gave the boys a book about becoming a Christian man. The book included a chapter condemning masturbation. While away at church college he was assigned to read another book, titled *Face Your Life With Confidence,* which included a chapter about masturbation called "I Have This Horrible Secret." In this way he was initiated into the sexual fears of our society.

Harold didn't date in high school, except for the juniors-Senior prom. That experience was quite awkward because he couldn't bring himself to hold hands and couldn't explain why to the girl, who was "just crushed." He had a few dates with girls in college, and his mother kept asking in her letters, "When are you going to marry?"

Harold went to graduate school and met a girl there who took an interest in him. They were engaged and married within a few months. They had two children, two years apart, but no sex after the birth of the second child. Nevertheless, they stayed together until she died at age fifty-six. She had chronic fatigue syndrome and fibromyalgia, so she would come home from work and collapse. That was convenient, in a way.

Homosexuality never came up specifically in Harold's church. Essentially, *anything* different was wrong—drinking, card playing, dancing. Harold remembers, "I felt so alone. I needed to talk to someone about the feelings I had, but there *wasn't* anyone."

Harold worked as a professional and formed a discreet relationship with another professional man, who was also married. They got together at conferences away from home. Meanwhile, Harold went to therapists, who helped him with his identity issues and more. Later he found a partner through a gay men's support group. He says today, "It's so hard to be okay with who you are, and not be accepted—or even be able to talk about it. I hope that the time will come that we can be accepted as persons."

Roxie, like Harold, grew up in a rural environment and attended an ethnic church. Her parents were alcoholic. Awareness of her sexual orientation came gradually. "I didn't have a word for it, but I remember having little dreams and fantasies when I was watching Annette Funicello on *The Mickey Mouse Club,*" from age five to nine. One dream she had at age eight was diving off the deck of a ship to save Annette, who was trapped fathoms below in a submarine. "I wanted to endear myself to her," says Roxie. A succession of crushes followed, on teachers, friends, camp counselors, even the principal's daughter. The fantasies, though, were romantic, not sexual.

In high school, a suspected lesbian relationship between two school staffers brought the idea of same-sex love into consciousness. Roxie had lots of overnights with friends, either singly or in groups. During a wrestling match with a friend she felt some arousal and asked herself in her diary, "What is it that's different in the way I feel about Evelyn?" She did date some boys, but none "rang her bell." She knew "there was something different about me," but she also had crushes on some male teen idols.

In college back East, Roxie recalls she "carried a torch" for a guy, but that didn't go anywhere. She developed a crush on a sorority sister who was two years older, but it was some years before that was pursued any further. She had "the total college experience—academic, social, activist," but remained a virgin. Near the end of her senior year she was turned on to Christianity by Rachel, a tennis partner, and became a "Jesus freak." That was the beginning of a lifetime faith journey, which would also be a journey of her sexual identity.

Roxie was recruited into a cult whose founder hated gay people and regarded homosexuality as an abomination. She was sent as a missionary to Alabama for a year at the age of twenty-four, to recruit new followers. "Everything was going great," Roxie relates, "until Isabel came along. She was gay, out, and flirting outrageously." Roxie was attracted to her and experienced "cognitive dissonance" between her emotions and her beliefs. The cult exercised strong control and tried to dissuade her from identifying as lesbian. When Isabel left town, Roxie started going to a lesbian bar, the only place she could find community. Thus she entered a "wild period" of drinking and promiscuity and experienced "the underbelly of gay life."

In the years following, Roxie alternated between sublimating her sexual feelings and denying her relationship with Christ. She came back to the Midwest, took more college courses, and was encouraged to go to graduate school. She became involved in a charismatic group. She had affairs and infatuations, but no true love. Then she met Monica at a party and the next day at a potluck. They both felt an immediate attraction. Monica had been married and divorced. They have now been together for fourteen years. Their experience illustrates the joke: "What do lesbians do on their second date?" Answer: "They move in."

Roxie had vowed that she would never come out to her parents, at least until she found someone. Her father died before she met Monica. Her mother came to love Monica. Another conflict, though, was looming again: sexuality versus spirituality. Roxie became enamored with a new church, which insisted that she remain celibate as a condition of being in good standing with God and the Church. She wanted to continue her relationship with Monica, but as a friend and soulmate only. She honored her church's requirement and withdrew from physical intimacy, while continuing to share a home with Monica. This went on for two years and took quite a toll on Monica.

For her part, Monica was in her mid-thirties before she realized that she preferred relationships with women. She had been married for seven years and had a daughter, but was divorced long before she understood her sexual orientation. In her first relationship with a woman, "it felt like a huge wall came down that I hadn't even realized I had put up." It was a big relief, and she "wanted to tell everybody." Sex was now taken out of the equation with respect to men, and that actually made it easier to be friends with them.

Her first woman lover urged caution, so Monica did not tell her family immediately. When she did, she found them to be accepting. Although she has relatives who are clergy, she has not been involved with the Church, except briefly in high school, and has never had a very positive image of the Church because of its patriarchal character. Hearing that someone is a "Christian" puts her immediately on guard, "because they may hate me. They either want to change you or see you dead."

When Roxie withdrew from physical intimacy, Monica was devastated. She cried and went to counseling, but after two years knew that she couldn't continue that way. When it came to the crunch, Roxie finally chose Monica over church. The effects, however, still linger. Roxie hasn't found a church yet that she can really respect that will also accept her relationship; and Monica, although she is "starting to mellow" toward church, still fears that her partner may one day be pulled away again.

What Monica would like to tell the wider Church is "how much harm they have done, beginning with special privilege. How you treat people is the important thing, not following the rules." She asserts that the Church "uses fear of death to keep people in line."

Society, also, is heterosexist, according to Monica.

> Every time you meet someone, they assume you are heterosexual. So you have to decide to come out—again and again and again. And this is stressful, because you're continually back in the closet, having to be on guard again.

Gay people also often put one another in the closet, with messages of "be careful."

Wendy, a lesbian who is now in a committed relationship, has been, like Rory, "one of the lucky ones." Growing up, she was surrounded by her mother's faith, even though she was not herself involved with the Church. In this way she picked up a view of God as accepting and loving. While her own trip has been smooth, she has seen gay friends who were disowned by their families. She sees a lot of discrepancy between the rhetoric of Christians and how they treat people.

Fred is a gay man who has faced a double challenge. After a socially awkward adolescence and a stint in the Marine Corps, he began to experience seizures. In his early thirties he was diagnosed with schizophrenia. He finally found a stable relationship through a gay men's support group, where he met Harold. He continues to live alone, supported by his friends and his medication.

Fred was lucky in that he wasn't readily identified as gay, only as shy. He has not been hassled as some of his friends have been. His family has been understanding, as well. What he has heard from the Church, however, has not been helpful. The message he gets from Evangelicals is, "You can be part of the Church, but you have to be celibate." What he would like to tell the Church is that some views of family "write him out." He does see some growing toleration in society toward gays, and he hopes that will continue "until we are seen as equals."

How does the view look from the other side of the fence, that is, from heterosexuals in the Church? Daniel, a retired professional and active church member, says: "I'm not sure that I was ever vociferously antigay. I didn't have to do a 180 degree turn; I just needed to become more aware. . . . There are three factors that helped me grow in my understanding of gay people."

The first, says Daniel, was a reassessment of holy scripture, influenced by several scholars and by his priest. Daniel amplifies:

> We have been wrong about how we have used scripture. We have used words to substitute for the Word. We have allowed fidelity to the words of scripture to make us deaf to the living

word who is among us . . . . It surprised me to discover that
Jesus never said anything about homosexuality.

When Daniel had struggled, years before, with the issue of
whether women should be ordained to the priesthood, a former
priest asked him if he believed in the Holy Spirit, and if so,
whether the Holy Spirit may influence the Church in such matters.
Daniel then realized that "the Church has been wrong before"—
about the shape of the universe and about slavery. Scripture, he has
come to see, "is not God's final word."

The second factor in Daniel's growth was "through people
I have gotten to know." He learned that a respected colleague
and church members he esteemed were gay. These people were
gifted, yet were regarded as being on the margin. Daniel admits,
"This was a humbling discovery, that I had undervalued gay
people."

The third element of his expanded awareness had to do with
equal rights. Through his family's own experience as immigrants,
he knew something about discrimination, which he says "is not
only un-American, it's un-Christian." He has come to regard his
earlier prejudices, such as the one against women in holy orders,
as unjust and unfounded. He sums up his current view in this way:
"I am in the process of freeing myself from the shackles of misin-
terpreting scripture and not knowing people as I ought. I am experiencing more freedom—and that is in tune with the Gospel."

Another longtime church member and leader is Bruce, who first
became aware of his *heterosexual* orientation at age twelve or thir-
teen. While not seen as "robust" by his male peers as he grew up,
Bruce found a sanctuary at the university high school, where he
hung out with a congenial coed group. He recalls no awareness of
gay or lesbian people in those years.

His exposure to how those outside the mainstream of society are
treated was increased through his experience driving a cab after
flunking out of college in his junior year—quite a comedown from
having been valedictorian of his high school class. One day after
a winter snowstorm he made the mistake of giving a little girl a
ride home by herself. When her mother complained and he was

reprimanded, Bruce learned how cab drivers were looked upon in society.

In the Army, Bruce became aware of sexual and racial discrimination. He chose not to date, even while overseas, and remained single after returning to civilian life. A case of mumps at age twenty had rendered him sterile, so he thought, "What's the point of dating?" Later he was married for a while.

What changed Bruce's mind about gays in the Church, despite a lingering visceral aversion to the idea of gay sex? It was a gradual process. He had himself felt like an outsider many times in his life. When he came out against the injustice of discrimination, he found his siblings hostile toward his liberal view. He says,

> I'd like the Church to know that God is love and loves all creatures. It's part of our human condition that not everyone is straight—and in the animal kingdom, also. The Church too often sacralizes prejudice. Those who should be the leaders fall in step and go along on this issue.

Sharon, now co-mothering a child with her partner Wendy, wants to tell the Church:

> Every human being deserves the right to have faith, to have a God . . . and to know that she is a child of God. Look at what Jesus did in his life, and how he treated everyone. . . . those who were condemned by the priests were treated [by Jesus] with love.

Doug asks church members to "reflect on what being heterosexual means to you. It's not all about the sex act." He poses the question: "Could anybody pray you or educate you into being gay?" "We gay people," he says, "have had lots of heterosexual teachers, yet we're still gay. The more I learn about what God and Jesus are really about, the more wrong I see that it is for gay people not to be included." He adds, "It wasn't that long ago that slavery was justified on the basis of the Bible. We've come to understand that slavery is wrong, but it's in the Bible, all over the place." In addition, we no longer condemn money-lending with interest, which is a big change from what the Bible says.

Doug has chosen to be a Christian and has worked at understanding God's will for him. He has a spiritual director. In order to stay sober and to grow as a Christian, he takes part regularly in many church-related groups in addition to Alcoholics Anonymous. He says, "Christianity is my foundation, and everything else comes out of that."

Meanwhile, Michael is estranged from his Church, which worked so hard to change him and has never accepted him as he is. What he wants to tell the Church is:

> They need to understand that there are alternative ways to read the Bible. Asking someone to change his sexuality is like asking someone to shed his skin. Gay people are not monsters, not evil, not perverted. Gay people would like to have a spiritual life, but feel they can't. We have a lot to offer.

Frank echoes that, saying, "I feel discrimination from the Fundamental Religionists and the meanness they spew forth. I believe intelligent people can see through their selective Bible quotations." His partner, Kevin, notes that they recently visited a church where the guest presider, a retired priest, told the congregation that he prayed he would never have to perform a marriage of two homosexuals—he didn't know if he could do it. As he looked out over the aging congregation, Kevin realized that it is God who is changing the church, even though it may be by "taking old bigoted thinking out of the Church one death at a time."

Kevin warms to the topic of prejudice.

> As a white man, presumed heterosexual for at least a part of my life, I stood up for the rights of minority races. I stood up for the rights of women. I could never understand why some people hated the Jews. . . . I understood when some people had to divorce their mates and start a hopefully better new life. . . . I am said to be a person with empathy—I can actually feel what others feel, and many times I don't like it. Are heterosexual Christians so unempathetic that they cannot even begin to feel the hurt we receive from their ignorance and noninclusion? And trust me on this—it hurts even more when the groups of people I have always tried to welcome

into my community don't want me a part of theirs. . . . Christ teaches us to forgive, not just once but seven times seven, or is it seventy times seven? It is so very hard to forgive people who have been unforgiving to us. Gay people have had to learn to be tolerant of others, we've learned the golden rule well, we smile and make a joke. We silently stand by as our fellow gays did in concentration camps and gas chambers in World War II Germany. You have asked about experiences of other gay people. One thing stands out, and that is the number of gay people who consider the Church their enemy. Many, and I mean many, will never forgive the Church for the way they have been treated. The Church is an important part of Frank's and my life. We talk about what happened or was said in church on a daily basis. A phenomenal number of times, gay people have confronted us on why we continue to be part of an organization that is openly trying to harm us. Without the Christian religion in the United States, there are no reasons . . . to hate gays. It is the basis or excuse most antigay people use.

Kevin has been reading the Bible a lot lately, and he says,

The Bible can be interpreted a million ways—I think it is time that it is interpreted from a gay point of view. For every verse that people use against us, there are ten verses about people who use God to put down others.

Some passages that Kevin might have cited include the following. "You shall also love the stranger, for you were strangers in the land of Egypt" (Deut. 10:19; see also Exod. 22:21). "The Lord works vindication and justice for all who are oppressed" (Ps. 103:6). "Truly I tell you, just as you did it to one of the least of these who are members of my family, you did it to me" (Matt. 25:40; see also Matt. 25:45). "Woe to you, scribes and Pharisees, hypocrites! For you tithe mint, dill, and cummin, and have neglected the weightier matters of the law: justice and mercy and faith" (Matt. 23:23). "Why do you pass judgment on brother or sister? For we will all stand before the judgment seat of God" (Rom. 14:10). "And if I have prophetic powers, and understand all mysteries and all knowledge, and if I have all faith, so as to remove mountains, but do not have love, I am nothing" (1 Cor. 13:2). "For everything created by God is good, and nothing is to be rejected, provided it is received with thanksgiving" (1 Tim. 4:4). "Blessed are you when people hate you, and when they exclude you, revile you, and defame you on account of the Son of man" (Luke 6:22). "We know that we have passed from death to life because we love one another. Whoever does not love abides in death" (1 John 3:14).

To the Church and to the world Kevin says,

> I'm a human being. I have feelings. I have something to offer and I do [offer it] despite your trying to keep me in my place . . . I'm tired of being treated [as] inferior to you. You are not better than me, you are not worse than me. You have dirt in your backyard, too. I would not change places with any of you. You would be happier if you would just accept and learn to be the person God made you. I am a child of God, too—how dare you try to drive a wedge between God and his children?

Elena backs up many of Kevin's comments. She says,

> Healing needs to happen for those gays and lesbians who have been damaged by Christianity. . . . It is so incredible that homosexuals are told that Jesus finds them disgusting. If anyone can relate, Jesus can relate. Jesus doesn't find homosexuals disgusting; he knows what we are going through.

In a positive vein she asserts:

> These people [of the GLBT community] have been given an incredible gift. They have been given a love that requires bravery and sacrifice. The church has a lot to learn from people who have loved when it is hard and have given up a lot—such as friends and family.

She recalls that at one point she could have stayed in the closet and married the youth minister of her church. Then she would have had material security and the respect of society.

As much as gays and lesbians need healing from the Church, the Church needs healing from gay and lesbian people. Both sides have a lot to gain from each other. We have a lot of energy, and a real experience with love that requires something. That kind of bravery makes room for the Holy Spirit.

I don't think I need to add anything further to the eloquent words of my sisters and brothers in the Church, who are open to the Holy Spirit and have a prophetic voice akin to that of the writer of Revelation: "Let anyone who has an ear listen to what the Spirit is saying to the churches" (Rev. 2:7, 2:11, 2:17, 2:29, 3:6, 3:13, 3:22).

Yours in reflection and repentance,

Letter 8

What the Bible Really Says

Dear Bible Explorer:

You have probably heard one or more of your friends, or some religious authority, say something such as this: "The Bible tells us unequivocally that homosexual activity is wrong." Did you take their word for it? Did you trust that they were giving you the "facts"? Did you do any research to confirm it?

When someone makes that kind of statement to me, my response, either vocally or silently, is "Oh, *really?*" Of course, I have an advantage. Not only have I read the alleged proof texts, I have also had the benefit of studying the contexts, and I can tell you unequivocally, once you examine the contexts and assumptions of the biblical writers, the "proof " becomes shaky, indeed.

What I have to share isn't all that original, and it isn't all that complicated, but it might change your mind about "what the Bible says about homosexuality." Are you willing to have that happen? I'm guessing that probably you are, or you wouldn't have read this far.

What I propose to do is take each of the problematic texts in the order it appears. As noted previously, we won't have to spend any time in the Gospels, because homosexual activity wasn't of any evident interest to Jesus—unless you think that lust or licentious behavior or fornication are unique to gay people.

Before I get to the texts in question, I want to review what I think are some basic principles for reading the Bible and evaluating any part of it. First, you need to read the entire Bible. Only then can you begin to appreciate the principle of meaning related to context and how a part of the Bible may relate to the whole.

© 2006 by The Haworth Press, Inc. All rights reserved.
doi:10.1300/5661_08

Next, remember that the Bible, like the Church, is human as well as divine. The Bible was written by two communities of faith over roughly a millennium. Human authors wrote through the lenses of their own experiences, assumptions, and concerns. They were no doubt inspired, but they were not infallible, and their horizon was limited. We know things today that the biblical writers did not, and we certainly do not share all of their assumptions. We have to ask, when reading a particular passage, "How is our world different today from the world inhabited by the biblical writer?" For example, we know something today about the dynamics of addiction and not just the state of drunkenness. We know that bad things do happen to good people, and that not all rewards and punishments are dispensed fairly in this lifetime.

Third, in order to discern a human author's purpose in a particular passage of scripture, we need to look at the context—the larger text in which the passage is embedded, and the historical situation and concerns that are being addressed. We need to consider the likelihood that the concerns we, in our own time and culture, bring to the passage are not necessarily the concerns of the author. We also need to pay attention to the type of material we are reading. The Bible is not a single book, but a whole library of books, including poetry, legendary material from the oral tradition, and stories that make an important point but are not literally true in their details. All of these materials can be edifying, but they need to be read in light of other parts of the Bible, as well as in light of things we know from tradition and more recent experience.

Fourth, as we have learned in recent years in all areas of study—in the sciences as well as in the humanities—the thing being observed and evaluated is not independent of the observer. The answers you get from the Bible depend in large part upon the questions you are asking and upon the assumptions you are making. We read the Bible *interactively;* that is, we are speaking to the text, even while the text is speaking to us. A given text may have more than one possible meaning. On what basis do we choose one meaning over another? If we do not examine ourselves as well as the text, we may be in the same state as the person Jesus observed trying to remove a splinter from his neighbor's eye (Matt. 7:3, Luke 6:42).

Finally, how do we assess the Bible in relation to other ways that God addresses us? Is the Bible God's final word to us? If so, why do we now set aside many parts of it, such as the Jewish laws of ritual purity, as no longer applicable? Is everything in the Bible something we now approve? What about the slaughter of noncombatants? We may notice that it still happens today, but do we see it as God's will? Most of us would say no. We run the biblical texts through the filters of our Christian sensibility, which has been formed by more than simply the texts themselves. "The word of God" now centers for us on the person of Jesus—everything he taught, everything he modeled, including a willingness to be led by the Holy Spirit. The Bible is a way that God can address us, but it is not the only way. The Bible itself testifies to various ways God can get our attention and instruct us: dreams, a burning bush, the advice of a father-in-law (Jethro to Moses), the experience of going into the wilderness, or exile. God is still revealing truth and wisdom to us, through the real prophets of our own day, as well as through our inner voice and our corporate experience. As Jesus was fond of saying, "He who has ears to hear, let him hear" (Matt. 11:15). Tradition, which is our accrued corporate wisdom in the church, is still developing.

That is probably more than enough by way of a word of caution. So, what is the first text in the Bible that has been read as a condemnation of homosexual behavior? It is Genesis 19:1-29, the account of the visit of two angels to Lot and his family in Sodom. The background is that God has heard unspecified distressing things about the behavior of the inhabitants of Sodom and Gomorrah, and has revealed to Abraham what he plans to do about it (Gen. 18). The angels, who have first visited Abraham, are on a scouting mission for God, to see if things are as bad in Sodom as God has heard they are. Abraham intercedes for the city and secures a promise from God to spare it if ten righteous people can be found there. Unfortunately, Lot and his family do not add up to ten.

When the angels, appearing as men, arrive in Sodom and are greeted by Lot, he is hospitable to them, as his uncle Abraham had been. However, all the men of Sodom surround Lot's house and demand that the visitors be brought out, so they can be raped. Lot pleads with them to desist, and if they insist on having someone to violate, he offers his virgin daughters as a substitute. (This story may be compared with Judges 19, where women are violated by the inhabitants of Gibeah in place of a visiting Levite, with dire consequences for that city.) Evidently, the requirement to extend hospitality to travelers in that time exceeded the requirement to protect one's own family. The angels intervene, and no violence is perpetrated. The next day, Lot and his family are evacuated, and the city is destroyed.

What is the sin of Sodom? Many readers of this account have assumed that it is homosexual behavior, but compare this story with what is reported to happen in some American prisons today, where vulnerable male prisoners are faced with a stark choice: either ally with a protector (who may demand sexual favors himself), or risk being assaulted indiscriminately. Are the perpetrators of such violence assumed to be homosexual? No, the crime is violence against persons; only the means is "sodomy." Similarly, in the Genesis account, the wickedness of the men of Sodom is seen as their malevolent intent toward visitors.

What else do we know about the people of Sodom, which might explain their condemnation? In Jeremiah 23:14, the adultery and lies of the prophets of Jerusalem are compared to Sodom and Gomorrah. In Ezekiel 16:49, the sin of Sodom is stated this way: "Behold, this was the guilt of your sister Sodom: she and her daughters had pride, surfeit of food, and prosperous ease, but did not aid the poor and needy." (Say what? This isn't sounding good for America today.) In the next verse, the prophet goes on: "They were haughty, and did abominable things before me; therefore I removed them, when I saw it." What might those "abominable things" have been? Our imagination may run riot—or does only one thing come to mind? The next verse continues, as the prophet is speaking to Jerusalem: "Samaria has not committed half your sins; you have committed more abominations than they, and have made your sisters appear righteous by all the abominations which you have committed."

Ezekiel really throws that word "abomination" around a lot, doesn't he? To what sins might he have been referring? When we examine the books of Exodus, Leviticus, and Deuteronomy, we find the word "abomination" applied to all the following behaviors: eating the flesh of a peace offering on the third day (Lev. 7:18); eating swarming things (Lev. 11:41)—an exception is made for locusts, crickets, and grasshoppers (Lev. 11:22); eating any aquatic creature without fins or scales ((Lev. 11:10); sacrificing an animal with a blemish or defect (Deut. 17:1); soothsaying and divining (Deut. 18:10); remarrying a defiled woman (Deut. 24:4); idolatry (Deut. 17:3-4); and cross-dressing (Deut. 22:5). Interestingly enough, the list of behaviors deemed worthy of a curse in Deut. 27:15-26 does not include a male lying with a male or a female lying with a female.

The word "abomination" pops up in many other places, notably in Proverbs, where it is applied to "lying lips" (12:22), the proud in heart (16:5), the scorner (24:9), the unjust man (29:27), and a whole litany of offenses (6:16-19), including haughty eyes, hands that shed innocent blood, a false witness, and one who sows discord. All this tends to raise a question: Why should one abomination be singled out above all the others? The issue in this and so many other instances where scripture is cited to convict someone of sin is not the citing of scripture but *how* a particular passage is used, especially when it is lifted from its context, while so many other passages that would help to provide a context are ignored.

This question is especially pertinent when we come to the two references to homosexual behavior in Leviticus: 18:22 and 20:13. The literal translation of the first is (no male shall) "lie the lyings of a woman." This is not a moral violation but a violation of purity according to the Hebrew thinking of that time: one's maleness is compromised (diluted, polluted) when one assumes the woman's role in the sexual act. It is akin to mixing two kinds of seed in a field or two kinds of fiber in cloth—behaviors which are also ruled out. Jesus rejected the principle of ritual cleanliness as our guide in making moral decisions, and so, in fact, do we.

In the second of these verses, Leviticus 20:13, the death penalty is prescribed to underline the seriousness of the offense. We should note, however, that the death penalty is also prescribed for adultery (Lev. 20:10); incest (Lev. 20:12); bestiality (Lev. 20:15 and Ex. 22:19); wizardry and sorcery (Lev. 20:27 and Ex. 22:18); blasphemy (Lev. 24:16); murder (Lev. 24:17); violating the Sabbath (Ex. 31:14); false prophecy (Deut. 13:5); idolatry (Deut. 13:6-9); being a rebellious son (Deut. 21:18-21); being not a virgin when married, if female (Deut. 22:20-21); and having sex with one who is betrothed, with special provisions if the female was in open country where her cries for help would not be heard (Deut. 22:23-25).

More pertinent than these matters of perspective is the context in which male homosexual behavior was viewed: it was seen as a participation in the Canaanite fertility rites with male shrine prostitutes, as can be seen in Leviticus 18:3: "You shall not do as they do in the land of Canaan." It is therefore not legitimate to extract these two verses in Leviticus as an absolute prohibition against homosexual behavior in all circumstances, since the context presumes religious meanings peculiar to that time and place, namely, an insistence on ritual purity and a rejection of pagan fertility practices.

The book of Leviticus knows nothing and cares nothing about a possible union between two males that could be an expression of love, caring, and faithfulness—such as the love between David and Jonathan (cf. 2 Sam. 1:26). Leviticus is focused solely on the assumptions and conditions of that society, which included not only many peculiar provisions for maintaining reverence, but also a relative contempt for women as the weaker sex. If you doubt that, please read through various battle situations in the Old Testament, and note the number of instances in which those who show fear or weakness in the face of a formidable foe are said scornfully to have "become as women."

With the consideration of these brief references in Genesis and Leviticus, we have exhausted what the Old Testament has to say about homosexual behavior. We turn now to the writings of St. Paul, beginning with the passage on which most of the weight of antigay sentiment in the Church has come down: Romans 1:26-27.

Paul is writing about the world's need for salvation, and he backs that up by listing all sorts of behaviors he sees as rebellious and depraved, including covetousness, malice, envy, murder, strife, deceit, gossip, slander, insolence, haughtiness, and disobedience to parents (Rom. 1:29-30). Sexual behavior that he assumes to be unnatural is added to his list as a fall from grace, which leads to the verses in question:

> God gave them up to dishonorable passions. Their women exchanged natural relations for unnatural, and the men like-wise gave up natural relations with women and were con-sumed with passion for one another, men committing shame-less acts with men and receiving in their own persons the due penalty for their error.

Here there is no mention of male-female orgies, since that kind of lust is "natural." In other words, Paul assumes that all people are by nature heterosexual. If they act upon same-sex attraction, it means something is wrong, and he presumes it is their religion. If they had been honoring their creator, they would not be going off the deep end and committing "shameless acts."

Paul is laying a foundation here for an exposition of the Gospel, since there is no need for an answer to a question that hasn't been asked. The punch line for the first three chapters of Romans is to be found in 3:23-24: "Since all have sinned and fall short of the glory of God, they are justified by his grace as a gift, through the redemption which is in Christ Jesus. . . ." Paul is heading toward good news, but first he has to give us the bad news, which is how messed up we are, both those living within Jewish law and those outside it.

An interesting sidelight to his line of reasoning is to be found in Romans 2:1, where he says: "Therefore you have no excuse, O man, whoever you are, when you judge another; for in passing judgment upon him you condemn yourself, because you, the judge, are doing the same things." I can hear the retort forming in some minds: "Wait a minute! I'm not gay, and I'm not doing those things!" Such a retort, of course, misses the point of what Paul is doing in his long list of offenses, which is establishing that no moral high ground exists upon which any of us can stand. So why would we single out one behavior above all the others? Could it be that we are heterosexist without noticing?

Just as in Leviticus, Paul makes reference to pagan rituals (Rom. 1:23) as examples of how people are led astray from honoring the one true God. For him, as for the Hebrews, "unnatural" sexual practices are linked to false religion. He does not conceive the possibility that someone might be created gay and might honor God by accepting that as a sacred trust, just as we heterosexuals accept our sexual nature as an energizing and potentially creative gift, though not without some hazards.

The only other references to homosexual behavior in the New Testament are two lists of unrighteous practices, one in 1 Corinthians and one in 1 Timothy. The former was certainly written by Paul, the latter more likely by one of his disciples.

The reference in 1 Corinthians 6:9, on a list of those who "will not inherit the kingdom of God"—including idolaters, adulterers, thieves, the greedy, drunkards and revilers—is to male prostitutes ("effeminate" in the King James Version) and those who patronize them ("abusers of themselves with mankind"). What is being condemned is sexual exploitation, on the part of the one taking advantage and the one allowing it. As Paul explains more fully in a discussion of prostitution in 1 Corinthians 6:15-20, something holy is debased in sex where one person is simply using another for gratification, with no love involved. What Paul does not imagine is the possibility that two same-sex partners *could* love each other, just as heterosexual couples might.

The author of 1 Timothy declares that

> the law is not laid down for the just but for the lawless and disobedient, for the ungodly and sinners, for the unholy and profane, for murderers of fathers and murderers of mothers, for manslayers, immoral persons, sodomites, kidnappers, liars, perjurers, and whatever else is contrary to sound doctrine. . . . (1 Tim. 1:9-10)

There you have it. The prosecution rests. If one commits sodomy, he is in pretty bad company. That is also the last word the New Testament has to say about homosexual behavior. Again, the assumption is: it's unnatural, therefore an offense against the creator and the moral order, and only low-life scum would participate in such a vile practice.

What does the Bible have to say about homosexuality? The first and shortest answer is: *nothing.* The Bible says nothing about homosexuality, because the Bible doesn't know anything about homosexuality as an orientation. It knows only about certain perverted practices in situations such as homosexual rape, temple prostitution, and the use of call-boys. These practices are seen as pretty well exhausting the possibilities for same-sex expression of desire, and are condemned as indicative of religious defects on the part of the perpetrators, who are acting against their presumed nature and in defiance of God.

What does the Bible have to say about homosexuality? If by homosexuality you mean homosexual behaviors, *not much.* Only two books in the Old Testament address the topic, one in the context of an inhospitable city, another in the context of an outdated code of religious purity. Only Paul in the New Testament addresses the topic, and then only in the contexts of idolatry and prostitution. If we come to any of these texts assuming that homosexual acts are unnatural, as Paul did, or wrong in every context, we have imported into the Bible a circular reasoning that makes these texts meaningless as "proof." If we do not import these assumptions, we are left with scant evidence that would justify condemnation of homosexual behavior as always wrong. In short, as the Bible frequently gives witness, sin is in the eye of the beholder.

If we come to the Bible for guidance on how to use the sexuality we have been given, we will find abundant counsel, following the main themes of stewardship and love that run throughout the Bible. We are not to exploit or abuse others in the pursuit of our sexual gratification; we are to respect the dignity of others, whether they are male or female, powerful or powerless; and we are to be supportive, as St. Paul so often urges, of those loving behaviors that build up the community and honor the goodness of the creator. Can we include faithful same-sex relationships in that recognition? I think we can.

Yours in telling it like it is,

Letter 9

From Being to Doing

Dear Person Trying to Do the Right Thing:

Can we adopt the assumption that nearly everyone wants to do the right thing? The problem is not always a lack of willpower, but often a matter of being conflicted in the face of differing advisors. In this chapter I will suggest some principles that may be helpful in making ethical decisions consistent with what we say we believe.

Christian ethics begins where every other ethics begins, with a view of reality. As we used to say in philosophy: "Every ethics presupposes a metaphysics." In other words, we can't decide what we ought to do until we have decided what is real. Many people today would like to dispense with religion and just talk about values, but one thing religion offers is a view of what is ultimately real. Free-floating values are like a plant with its roots plucked out of the soil. In the long run, that plant is going to lack nourishment; it cannot endure, let alone thrive, without the nurturing soil of belief.

For Christians, our metaphysics is to be found in the Apostles' Creed and Nicene Creed, with their central focus on the incarnation, death, and resurrection of Jesus the Christ. It is not just his earthly life and teaching but also his death and resurrection that give us our vision of reality, our pattern of life as God intends for us, our hope for a life with ultimate meaning, and our commission as ethical beings. Because Jesus died and rose again, we are empowered to live as stewards of God's vision and gifts in this world. The dream that would otherwise be a fantasy—that we might give ourselves fully without losing ourselves and that we might become truly one with God, in spite of our shortcomings—is now a

doi:10.1300/5661_09

91

real and inviting possibility. Because we are secure in our union with Christ, we are free like the man of La Mancha to "march into hell for a heavenly cause."

If no life exists beyond this one, we are not so free to risk the only life we have. Fear, rather than love, then tends to rule our lives. Everything is then measured in terms of "What's in it for me?" However, "perfect love casts out fear" (1 John 4:18). When we know that God is committed to us, and that the only fatal mistake we could make would be not to trust him, we are free to follow the leading of love and to be less motivated by the sanctions of this world. We are free to risk as Jesus risked, speaking the truth even to those who have power to hurt us. Our vision is that their power is limited. We trust in a power that exceeds those limits.

Our ethics, therefore, is an ethics of thanksgiving. It is an ethics of relationship. Because our lives are ultimately secure in Christ and we are members of his body, we have already lost our lives and gained eternal life. All that remains for us is to express our gratitude and our trust in him. Christian ethics begins with the knowledge that we are forgiven sinners with a heavenly destiny, called to live by grace. We do not have to prove ourselves worthy of God's love; we have been declared worthy, as the voice came from heaven at the baptism of Jesus: "You are my Son, the Beloved; with you I am well pleased" (Mark 1:11).

The pattern of St. Paul's epistles is metaphysics, then ethics. Here is the good news, Paul says. Here is the foundation. Now, what are you going to build upon it? The pattern is most explicit in 1 Corinthians 3:10-15:

> According to the grace of God given to me, like a skilled master builder I laid a foundation, and someone else is building on it. Each builder must choose with care how to build on it. For no one can lay any foundation other than the one that has been laid; that foundation is Jesus Christ. Now if anyone builds on the foundation with gold, silver, precious stones, wood, hay, straw—the work of each builder will become visible, for the Day will disclose it, because it will be revealed with fire, and the fire will test what sort of work each has

done. If what has been built on the foundation survives, the builder will receive a reward. If the work is burned up, the builder will suffer loss; the builder will be saved, but only as through fire.

This is our guarantee, our challenge, and our commission. Our works are meaningful and will be reviewed at the end of our lives. The works that are seen to be worthy will endure and be recognized. Those that were done for earthly gain will not survive the purifying fire of God's perfect love, but as long as we are standing on the foundation of Jesus Christ, we ourselves will not be destroyed; we are saved by grace though faith, not by our works.

Our ethics, therefore, is not about earning anything, but about remaining true to the precious gift of love we have received. Our ethics is not primarily about following a set of rules, but honoring the spirit and vision of our leader and savior. Our ethics centers in the person of Jesus—his teaching and his example. We are called to give witness with our lives to the preaching he practiced.

What, then, is the place of the Ten Commandments? Unlike the ceremonial law and much of the case law of the old covenant that has been set aside as inapplicable in the New Testament, the Ten Commandments are still in force. When Jesus said (Matt. 5:17), "I have come not to abolish but to fulfill the Law," he was pointing to the love that transcends and transforms law and license. Law says, "Your acceptance by God is conditional." License says, "God doesn't care what you do, so you can do anything you please." Love says, "God cares so much that he sent his only son—to set you free from rebellion and fear, so that you can serve someone besides yourself, because now you know that you are loved."

When a lawyer asked Jesus (Luke 10:25), "Teacher, what must I do to inherit eternal life?" Jesus turned the question back at him, and the lawyer offered a summary of the Ten Commandments: "You shall love the Lord your God with all your heart, and with all your soul, and with all your strength, and with all your mind; and your neighbor as yourself"(Luke 10:27). This was, Jesus said, the right answer; and it is so for us, as well. The important thing for us to see is that loving God and neighbor is not simply our call; it is our privilege and what we were created to do. We find our fulfillment in serving God, since we no longer have to secure our lives.

The Ten Commandments are like a protective boundary around the good life that God wants for us. The boundary is there to keep us from hurting ourselves and others, but the boundary itself cannot give us life. Life in its fullness comes from loving and being loved. It comes from receiving and giving, being thankful, and being generous. It comes not from proving anything, but from sharing everything.

In my second letter to you I discussed what Jesus does in the Sermon on the Mount: far from lowering the bar for Christians, he raises it so that we come to see the impossibility of justifying ourselves or living by force of will rather than by grace. He says, for example (Matt. 5:27-28): "You have heard that it was said, 'You shall not commit adultery.' But I say to you that everyone who looks at a woman with lust has already committed adultery with her in his heart." Not only our actions but also our most private thoughts and feelings are important.

If we had to be innocent in order to be approved by God, every one of us would be in big trouble. Fortunately, the Gospel has a different message: you are guilty, but also forgiven; now go and live in the power of that forgiveness. The message we get from the culture, however, is not the same as the good news of Jesus. In our binary-thinking culture, where we are continually sorting things into categories for convenience, shades of gray are generally seen as moral compromise or "fuzzy thinking"; right and wrong are supposed to be black and white. It would be nice if our individual consciences could tell us unerringly what to do in every situation, but conscience is not only religiously influenced, it is also culturally shaped. Our Christian ethics need to be in dialogue with our consciences, but also with the Gospel.

How do we know what is the right thing to do in a given situation? Besides accepting that we will not always be right, we need to recognize that no set of principles will give us explicit guidance in every situation. We do well to take into account principles such as respect for the autonomy of persons, seeking to avoid doing harm, striving for justice for all, and seeking to be faithful to promises. The central principle for Christians, around which these other principles cluster, is the command to love expressed in the golden rule ("Do unto others as you would have them do unto you"—Luke 6:31), the summary of the law (expressed by the lawyer in Luke 10), and supremely in the example of Jesus.

Now we reframe the question: How do we know what is the loving thing to do in a given situation? We have the model of Jesus, and we can pray for guidance, but we do not have the benefit, as did the first disciples, of a face-to-face dialogue with our Lord based on the particulars of the situation that confronts us, though we may have the shared wisdom of a community. What we can do, in seeking to do the loving thing toward our neighbor, is to find out what our neighbor needs. This is not necessarily identical with what our neighbor wants, but neither can it be learned independently of dialogue with our neighbor. We may think we know what our neighbor needs, but until we have engaged our neighbor and learned something of what it is like to be in his or her shoes, we are not in a position to make a sound ethical decision.

Before we can truly love our neighbor, therefore, we have to get to know our neighbor. Good intentions and warm feelings are not enough. Love is primarily a verb, requiring one to: ask, listen, explore, study, empathize, identify, accompany. Unless we do the work of getting to know our neighbor, we may be complicit in injustice without knowing it. The founding father of general semantics, Alfred Korzybski, was fond of saying, "The map is not the territory," meaning that you may have an idea in your head (in this case concerning what it is like to be another person, and what principles should govern your action toward that person), but when you get down "on the ground" (with that other person) you are likely to find that the reality of the "terrain" is more complicated than your "map" represented. It is fine to have ideals; it is important also to know what is actually happening.

Here is where it is important to have dialogue beyond our comfortable inner circle of friends with closely similar experiences and opinions. Instead of building communities of agreement but limited vision, we need to see the entire human family as linked despite the cacophony of competing hopes and agendas. The love that Jesus taught and exemplified is a giving of self for all others, not just a select few. If God loves all people, then that is our call as well. We will not find our salvation by separating ourselves from the rest of humankind.

Although ethical decision making must be based on ideals that are generalizable, it cannot lose sight of the particulars. A rule that works well for many may be terribly unjust for a few. Before we accept that injustice may be simply "collateral damage" justified by our main objective, we should ponder the teachings of Jesus about a God who notices when even a sparrow falls to the ground (Matt. 10:29) and a shepherd who leaves the many to go in search of the one who is lost (Luke 15:4). Seldom do we have the luxury of choosing between two courses of action where there is not a "down" side as well as an "up" side to each. Before dismissing the "down" side as unavoidable, we had better get a little closer to it. When we do, we may find that it is not so easy to dismiss.

For example, the Church for many years treated divorced persons as second-class citizens and justified that treatment on the grounds that we needed to discourage divorce. The problem was that, for many people, divorce represented a more lifegiving choice than remaining in a destructive marriage. Many people who found themselves divorced despite their best efforts suffered discrimination at the hands of a church and of its members, who were very sure they were doing the right thing.

Just as context is important when we are assessing the significance of a Bible verse, context is vital when we are deciding what is the loving thing to do. Before we justify enforcing a policy in the name of "tough love," we should imagine ourselves in the position of someone for whom the policy is an injustice. I remember well two foreign graduate students, husband and wife, who were deported and all their educational investment aborted when their support from their home country proved inadequate and the husband took a part-time job. When I appealed to the regional director of the Immigration and Naturalization Service on their behalf, I was told: "Sorry. They broke the rule, and that's it." It is easy enough to understand where the director was coming from—how could he make an exception for them without opening the door to a flood of other such requests? No doubt he is overworked and understaffed as it is. However, his response falls far short of justice, in that it takes no account of the disproportionate nature of the penalty, given the size of the investment and the effect upon this family.

In the real world, we cannot always foresee what preventive measures should have been taken. In the real world, some people get pregnant despite their best intentions, some budgets come up short, some good people find themselves in no-win situations through no fault of their own. It is easy in such situations to distance ourselves and say, "Well, surprise!—life isn't fair!" It is more loving, however, to look at the particulars of the situation and to see if a remedy can be found.

A Christian ethics worthy of the name does not begin by making pronouncements, but by seeking to get closer to the situation, in order to ask first, "What is going on?" When God took human flesh, a powerful statement was made about God's disposition toward us. God said, in effect,

> I'm not going to judge you from afar or save you from afar. Instead, I will come among you and live as one of you, in order to break down that wall between us. I am willing to get dirty and to suffer so that you may know me, and to show you that I love you.

Our Christian journey in this life is an exercise in growing a character that is more Christlike, as well as one of learning to live in a community of imperfect neighbors. The ethical decisions we make along the way are not primarily a means of saving ourselves—God has saved us, after all—but a matter of coming to recognize our connection with an extended family. In that light, it is not sufficient to look only at the end to be served; we must come to see that every human being is a precious child of God, not expendable merely to achieve a worthy goal.

In order to live in community we may have to get our hands dirty, as God was willing to be born in a stable and to lie in a feeding trough. When we choose people for positions of leadership, we recognize that we are entrusting to them the difficult task of making decisions with which we will not always agree—decisions between the lesser of evils, decisions which will be scrutinized and criticized by the community at large. We try to choose persons who are enlightened and courageous, not just self-serving, for that difficult task of discernment and commitment in service of the community. "Politics," it has been said, "is the art of compromise," but how we need and cherish, if only in retrospect, those leaders who are willing to do the unpopular but necessary thing, even at the cost of losing their offices. So as we act as stewards of God's world, we need to be looking toward our Lord more than toward the current opinion polls. What *would* Jesus do? That's always a good question to ask and ponder before we leap to the conclusion that we already know the answer.

It's tempting but dangerous to generalize from our own experience: how we went about getting a job, or raising a child, or holding a marriage together. It's especially hazardous to generalize when the playing field isn't level and one is a member of the privileged class, for whom the rules work pretty well. One question I have come to see as very important in any given situation is this: "What is this going to cost, and who will be paying the price?" I have learned to be leery of those who advocate a course of action in which they are differentially invested from others. For example, how many of those who advocate going to war have sons or daughters who will be among the first to go? How many of those who advocate a flat tax are living on extremely limited incomes? How many of those who advocate celibacy for some group in society are celibate themselves? How many of those who advocate doing away with government welfare payments are in the situation of a single mother with limited education and no access to child care? How many of those who advocate diminished support for the public schools have children in those public schools and have visited the schools to see all the demands upon the teachers? How many of those who deplore subsidizing the homeless are themselves receiving subsidies in terms of preferential tax treatment? The questions could go on.

A joke sums up the matter rather well. The farmyard animals were assembled, and each was exhorted to help put food on the farmer's table. The cow and the chicken said that was only fair and equitable. The pig, however, had an objection. "Easy for you to say!" observed the pig. "You're making a contribution; I'm being asked for a total commitment!"

The center of our Christian ethics is Jesus, "the man for others," the one who made a total commitment. When we look to him rather than to the norms of a particular culture, we are more likely to do the loving thing. The sad fact is that many of those who are quick to insist that "the majority rules" are not so quick to see or admit that the majority is not always right, not always loving. In my home state, 70 percent of the voters approved an amendment to the state constitution that singled out one group of citizens for unequal treatment. Gays and lesbians, according to this amendment (which is now being challenged in the courts), are not entitled to the legal benefits accorded to heterosexual couples, since the former are not entitled to marry. What justification was offered for this injustice? Only that full legal recognition of same-sex partnerships would undermine traditional (i.e., religious) views of marriage. No satisfactory evidence has been put forward that actual heterosexual marriages would be undermined. In fact, faithful same-sex unions may serve to inspire heterosexual couples who are tempted to bail out of marriage at the first crisis. Further, the more we study the history of marriage, the more variety we find. There is no historical or moral justification for sanctioning one contemporary and religious view of marriage at the expense of all others.

So what *are* the big ethical issues of our time? Although popular attention in the media is focused on how we handle public money and private sexuality, comparable attention is not paid to much larger issues such as: How are we caring for the environment, so as to provide for the generations to come? How are we addressing the growing gap between obscene wealth and abject poverty? How are we learning, in this global village, to live with diversity, especially religious diversity? How are we providing for the needy in our world today? How are we addressing the interlinked issues of population growth and sustainable development? How are we looking out for those who are readily seen by society as "dispos-able" because they have no influence—the forgotten incarcerated, the solitary and indigent aged, the invisible rural poor, the children without parents of means, the mentally ill (whether inside or out-side of institutions), and those who have been labeled as morally deviant because of their sexual orientation? Jesus is quoted as say-ing, "As you did it to one of the least of these who are members of my family, you did it to me" (Matt. 25:40).

Some of the major points I have tried to make in this letter, dear reader, include the following:

1. Christian ethics flows from our view of reality, which is centered in Jesus and the Trinity and rooted in the mystery of death and resurrection.
2. Christian ethics is an ethics of response and relationship, not of works done to earn favor with God.
3. Christian ethics encourages us to get our hands dirty and to live by grace, not to worry about being faultless.
4. Loving our neighbor as ourselves requires us to get close enough to know our neighbor and to see the entire human family as linked. Prejudice happens when we are distanced and do not understand what other people are facing.
5. The loving thing to do depends upon the reality of the par-ticular situation; we always need to ask first, "What is go-ing on?"
6. As we work on our ethics, we are working on ourselves, growing in character, becoming more Christlike.
7. Christian ethics challenges cultural norms and asks, "Who pays most?" Saying "majority rules" is inadequate.
8. The big ethical issues of our day have to do with our stew-ardship of shared resources, not just our private lives.
9. How we treat people is the real test of whether we are Jesus-centered.
10. Christian ethics is servant ministry, as I will now explain.

At the center of our Christian ethics is Jesus, the one who taught his disciples that a price is paid to follow him, and that "those who want to save their life will lose it" (Mark 8:35). "Whoever wants to be first must be last of all and servant of all," said Jesus (Mark 9:35). The mystery at the heart of our faith is not only that Jesus died and lives again but that we will find our lives as we surrender our lives in God's service. When Jesus gave his final address to his disciples in John 13, he took up not a lawbook but a basin and towel. May our ethics follow him.

Yours in the ministry of discernment, community,
and self-giving,

Letter 10

Appeal to the Bride of Christ

Dear Shaper of a Better Future:

Thanks for coming along with me on this journey of discovery. We met, we centered ourselves on Jesus and what love requires, and we took a look at how flawed we are as a church and as a culture, particularly in dealing with issues of sexuality. We heard from some people who formerly were silent. We took a look in context at the texts in scripture used to condemn homosexuals, and I outlined some principles for doing justice in the light of the Gospel. Now I offer you a word of encouragement for your continuing quest as a member of the Body of Christ.

Here are some things I have learned about GLBT people over the past fifteen to twenty years: As a group, they are no more sex-obsessed or predatory than the general population. They have the same general aspirations as heterosexuals. They want to develop their gifts, find rewarding employment, and live free of discrimination. They want to find someone to love and to form family units. They want to pursue the spiritual, intellectual, and artistic paths that nurture the human spirit. They want to contribute to church and society as respected citizens. Above all, they want to be free to be who they are, who they have come to accept that God created them to be: persons differently oriented with regard to affection and physical attraction, yet fully healthy in every way.

It is terribly sad that the greatest barriers to full inclusion of GLBT persons in our society have been erected by the Christian Church, that body charged with bearing the life-giving news of God's great love in Jesus. The Church has many corporate sins of

doi:10.1300/5661_10

which to repent, but in our day this one tops the list for sheer unapologetic meanness.

You will hear many Christians say, "Hate the sin, but love the sinner." Two things are wrong with this pious platitude. One is the easy acceptance of the canard that expressing one's sexuality as a homosexual in any way, shape, or form is somehow a blasphemy against God—without taking the trouble to assess the validity of a heterosexist cultural assumption in religious costume. The other is the lack of empathy and imagination to feel what it may be like to hear such a message, when one is powerless to change one's sexual orientation. Instead of the unconditional love of Jesus that the rest of us are privileged to hear as Good News from God, GLBT persons are asked to accept a second-class gospel of conditional love:

> You can be accepted by the Church and by God only if you *refrain* from acting upon your sexual feelings, even in a responsible way; if you embark on a program to *change* your feelings; or if you *hide* who you really are.

Gay and lesbian persons, with little or no encouragement and recognition of their loving relationships, have nevertheless persevered to form and maintain long-term unions that have put many of our heterosexual marriages to shame. Gay and lesbian persons have served honorably in the armed forces of our country, when they have been permitted to do so. They have held important political offices without incident of scandal. They have been creative artists and innovators, dedicated teachers, counselors, clergy, and good friends to many of us.

The gay people I know, both inside and outside the Church, exhibit stability, authenticity, courage, generosity, good humor, and great dedication in their lives and various callings. I will put their character and ethics up against those of anyone. How can the church, of all institutions, treat them as second-class citizens? How can the church continue to perpetuate discrimination based on fear and ignorance? How can we continue to betray the trust that Jesus has placed in us as bearers of the Good News of God's love for all persons?

Gay persons are not seeking to convert anyone. Being gay is not a "lifestyle," it is a matter of *being,* more than doing. Behavior is fluid, sexual orientation is not. It falls somewhere on a continuum and can only be expressed or repressed. Sexual behavior may be responsible or irresponsible—and that is true for all of us.

What stands in the way of changing the corporate mind of the Church? Obviously, tradition is a strong factor: it is very hard for the Church ever to admit that it has been wrong. As Peter Gomes has ably demonstrated in his 1996 work, *The Good Book: Reading the Bible with Mind and Heart,* the Bible has been used both as a text of liberation by oppressed peoples and as a text of subjugation by those who are quite comfortable with the current social arrangements. The Bible can be used either to reinforce tradition or to bring tradition more fully into line with the abiding truth of the Gospel.

In order to fulfill its mission of bringing the Gospel to all the world, the Church needs two poles for its orientation: one is the pole of conviction rooted in an eternal gospel, the other is the pole of openness to change in response to the leading of the Holy Spirit. Jesus lives in *both,* not just the former. When we cite Hebrews 13:8 ("Jesus Christ is the same yesterday and today and forever"), we surely do not mean that our understanding can never change, or that what is involved in being faithful to the Gospel never needs to be reexamined.

Why has the Church been so resistant to change? In the case of owning up to homophobia and the truth about homosexual people, one uncomfortable fact is that there has been no real reward in earthly terms (careers, success, and so on) for Christian leaders to confront popular prejudice. Taking the lead in suggesting that Jesus might not be so pleased about how we have treated our gay brothers and sisters has not been a politically advantageous position for anyone desiring to build consensus and gather support for church programs. In the face of so many other challenges to the contemporary Church, not the least of which is our fractured state on issues of sexuality and biblical interpretation, it has been far easier for leaders to go along with the maxim that "We cannot condone sin" than it would be to educate our people to read the Bible more comprehensively and courageously.

The Church today is divided on issues of authority, with some denominations or factions within denominations favoring strong pronouncements from the top down, others favoring grassroots mandates supposedly based on scripture, and still others favoring a more balanced basis of authority, looking not only to tradition and scripture but also to reflection upon contemporary experience and discernment of the Holy Spirit. The biggest source of division in the Church, however, is not the conflict between doctrines, as well-entrenched as these may be, but the disparity in life experience between those who remain shielded from injustice and suffering and would like their lives to go on in the same comfortable way and those who cannot insulate themselves from the injustice experienced by a gay or lesbian friend or family member.

Would you like to become more open to the needs and aspirations of gay persons? The best place to start is by getting to know the gay people who are already in your life. Commit yourself to being an ally and find out what kind of support is needed. In order to be more effective as an ally, educate yourself by reading and talking to people who know what it is like to suffer discrimination for their sexual orientation.

What is it like to be a disadvantaged minority? Perhaps you, dear reader, already know something about that. Perhaps you are a member of the clergy and know all the bad jokes and stereotypes that are still going around. Perhaps you are an introvert in a society that rewards extroversion. Perhaps you were a nerd in high school, as I was. Perhaps you were not blessed with social poise, or athletic talent, or good looks, or any of the assets that make life easier for a young person growing up. Perhaps you know how it feels to be misunderstood, to be "out of step" with most of the people around you. Perhaps you have been the butt of jokes because you didn't measure up in some ways.

Speaking personally, I do not credit myself for most of the good things in my life today, since I was favored as a white, male, heterosexual, Christian American with the opportunity to get a college degree. Although I have paid a lot of dues, including service in the armed forces, all of the good things I enjoy today have come my way by the grace of God, including faith, family, friends, material blessings, and meaningful work. I have been one of the lucky ones, despite feeling very lonely at times in my life. I am thankful, and I understand that the system in church and society has given me advantages not afforded to all others.

The Christian faith, as I understand it, is not primarily about earning status with God but about how we use the gifts that have been entrusted to us. How thankful and generous are we able to be? What leaps of faith are we willing to take for the sake of sharing the Good News? How accepting are we willing to be of those who are different from us? How far will we reach out to the less fortunate?

Although there are times when my faith as a Christian calls me to challenge some things my country does, one precious treasure has been entrusted to me as a member of a society committed to liberty that was first entrusted to me by the gift of Jesus Christ: the great privilege and responsibility of freedom. That sacred trust is stated very well in James 2:12: "So speak and so act as those who are to be judged by the law of liberty." Remember 1 Corinthians 3:10-15 and the life we build on the foundation of our acceptance and forgiveness in Jesus. Freedom is conferred to us not only by the U. S. Constitution but also by the God who created us and pronounced all creation as good (Gen. 1:31).

My freedom is a gift I believe I am called to help extend to the entire human family. That does not mean imposing American values upon others, but acting in ways that foster self-determination and development. As I look around at our world today, I see that sin continues to be rampant. Everywhere I look are expressions of selfishness, denial of responsibility for injustices, and the insistence upon personal comfort and security at the expense of others. Not only is there disregard for future generations but a hardness of heart and smallness of spirit is present among so many, especially those who, in the pursuit of their worship of false gods such as money and status, project their own darkness upon others. The sins that worry me most are not the "warm sins" of sex between consenting adults who are not married, but the "cold sins" of indifference to the suffering of others.

I am given some encouragement, as I also see around me many signs of faithfulness, public concern, and commitment to the common welfare. However, if we, the church, the bride of Christ, are to lead the way in shaping a better future, we need to return to our first love (Rev. 2:4), our devotion to a gospel that liberates and gives more abundant life to all, rather than seeking to control some so as not to inconvenience others. The Church needs to get back to her call of *living* the Good News, and for that she needs—*we* need—courage, love, and diligence in pursuit of the truth that can set us all free.

How do people change their minds with regard to prejudice? The best answer I know of is through human relationships, whereby fear and mistrust evaporate and are replaced with respect and affection. When we have become better educated through such relationships, we will begin to challenge the misapplication of the word "lifestyle" to denote sexual orientation. We will promote more opportunities for dialogue and probe more deeply into popular assumptions. We will become more aware of the social and psychological climate in which gay people live and ask ourselves whether that climate is as safe and healthy and truly Christian as it can be.

The great spiritual pilgrimage chapter of the Bible is Hebrews 11, wherein we read of the travails of our spiritual ancestors—some of the many who have made arduous life journeys in search of a place they could call home. As I read once again this moving account, I cannot help but think of the suffering of so many faithful gay Christians, of whom—to paraphrase—the world is not worthy. Christians such as Michael, who struggled for ten fruitless years to make himself acceptable, and Kevin, who has labored so long for the church only to find himself still stigmatized. I think also of the sufferings of our Lord Jesus, who must continue to look upon a world where so many of his sisters and brothers are unloved or unloving.

Our call, dear bride, if we are faithful to our vows, is as stated in Hebrews 13:13, "Let us then go to him outside the camp and bear the abuse he endured." For, just as those who came before us in the pilgrimage, "here we have no lasting city, but we are looking for the city that is to come" (Heb. 13:14).

It is important for us to be aware of and to confront our own fears. Are we afraid of befriending a gay person because of what our friends might think? Are we afraid of being labeled as "not Bible-believing" because we think the Bible is misused when it is applied so narrowly, inconsistently, and unlovingly? What do you think Jesus would say to us if we brought these fears to him?

God bless you, Christian bride, bearer of the Good News. You are the one who can make a difference in the communities of which you are a part. You hold the future of our Church and our world in your hands and in your heart. "Remember those who are in prison, as though you were in prison with them . . ." (Heb. 13:3) and take heart in the promise, as though you were a member of Lot's family, surrounded and besieged by those hostile to out-siders: "Do not neglect to show hospitality to strangers, for by doing that some have entertained angels without knowing it" (Heb. 13:2).

Yours in the ongoing quest for life and love for all,

Index

Abomination, 85
Addiction, sex as, 46
Apostolic, Church as, 37, 40
Appearance, elevation of, 13
Asexual, Church as, 46
Authority, Church divided on, 106

Baptism, 25, 35-36
Bawer, Bruce, 55
Being versus doing, 91-101
Bellah, Robert, 22
Bible, on homosexuality, 81-90
Biblical passages
    Colossians, 2:8, 21
    Colossians 2:16-17, 21
    Colossians 2:20-22, 21
    1 Corinthians 3:10-15, 92-93
    1 Corinthians 7:1, 49
    1 Corinthians 13:2, 78-79
    Deuteronomy, 85-86
    Deuteronomy 10:19, 78
    Ephesians 2:8-9, 20
    Ezekiel 16:49, 84
    Galatians 2:21, 19
    Galatians 3:28, 49
    Galatians 5:1, 19
    Genesis 1:27, 45
    Genesis 1:31, 45
    Hebrews 13:8, 105
    Hebrews 13:13, 108-109
    Hebrews 13:14, 109
    James 2:12, 107
    John 1:9, 14, 6
    John 14:9, 18
    John 17:21, 39

Biblical passages *(continued)*
    1 John 3:14, 79
    Leviticus, 85-86
    Luke 6:22, 79
    Luke 7:47, 15
    Luke 10:25, 15, 93
    Luke 10:27, 93
    Luke 10:29, 15
    Luke 10:36, 16
    Luke 10:37, 16
    Luke 15:2, 16
    Mark 1:11, 92
    Mark 7:6-8, 14
    Mark 7:14-15, 14
    Mark 7, 21-23, 14
    Mark 8:35, 100-101
    Mark 9:35, 101
    Mark 12:31, 27
    Matthew 5:20, 17
    Matthew 5:27-28, 94
    Matthew 5:48, 17
    Matthew 6:25-33, 17
    Matthew 7:11, 17
    Matthew 7:12, 17
    Matthew 23:23, 78
    Matthew 25:40, 78, 100
    Philippians 2:6-7, 20
    Philippians 2:12-13, 20
    Philippians 3:7-9, 20-21
    Psalms 103:6, 78
    Revelation 2, 80
    Romans 1:29-30, 87
    Romans 2:1, 87
    Romans 3:23-24, 87
    Romans 14:10, 78
    1 Timothy 1:9-10, 88
    1 Timothy 4:4, 79

doi:10.1300/5661_11